The Project Management Life Cycle

The Project Management Life Cycle

A complete step-by-step methodology for initiating, planning, executing & closing a project successfully

Jason Westland

London and Philadelphia

First published in Great Britain and the United States in 2006 by Kogan Page Limited

120 Pentonville Road
London N1 9JN
United Kingdom
www.kogan-page.co.uk

525 South 4th Street, #241
Philadelphia PA 19147
USA

© Jason Westland, 2006

British Library Cataloguing-in-Publication Data

A CIP record for this book is available from the British Library.

ISBN 0 7494 4555 6

Typeset by Saxon Graphics Ltd, Derby
Printed and bound in Great Britain by Cambridge University Press

Contents

Figures

Tables

Foreword

As a project manager, having to juggle staff, customers, suppliers, materials and equipment to deliver your project can be challenging. To succeed, you need to use a well structured methodology for initiating, planning, executing and closing projects effectively. Only a handful of best-practice project management methodologies exist in the market place, and few actually describe in any real detail how to complete every phase, activity and task. This book does exactly that.

Because it explains the entire project life cycle in detail, you will understand how to use simple, practical processes to successfully deliver your projects. Whether you intend to initiate, plan, execute or close a project, this book explains how to do it quickly and efficiently. *The Project Management Life Cycle* provides a comprehensive description for each of the 20 critical project activities, as well as more than 150 tables, diagrams, forms and checklists containing real-life examples to help you along the way.

This book reveals the Method123® Project Management Methodology (MPMM) which has been used by 45,000 people in more than 50 countries around the world. It has helped me personally to manage projects successfully, and I am sure it will help you to do so as well.

Pamela Good
Vice-President of Communications
Project Management Institute
Buffalo Chapter, USA

Preface

Over the past 20 years, businesses around the world have undergone rapid change. No longer are customers happy with their 'status quo' products or services: they expect businesses to adapt rapidly to the changing environment by providing more offerings, cheaper and faster than before. This rate of change has forced businesses to transform their operational processes into project-based initiatives. This transformation has not been without its risks, as a large percentage of projects (estimated by the Standish Group as more than 70 per cent) fail to deliver on time, on budget and to the level of quality expected.

Why such a large percentage of projects fail to deliver

Typical causes include poor project sponsorship, undefined requirements and miscommunication. However the number one cause of project failure is the lack of adoption of a formal project methodology. Without adopting a clear methodology or framework for delivery, most project teams start building deliverables before their scope and objectives are clearly thought through. They have no structured processes for undertaking project tasks, and so they fail to effectively manage time, cost, quality, risks, issues and changes within the project. It is inevitable that such projects suffer from scope creep, milestone delays, poor deliverable quality and a lack of customer satisfaction. The answer is simple: use a repeatable project methodology with structured project processes for initiating, planning, executing and closing projects effectively.

Which methodology to use

There is no clear answer. Few best-practice project management methodologies exist in the market place. Most self-professed methodologies are nothing more than a set of stages with a brief description for each stage. During 12 years of research and managing projects, the only comprehensive project management methodologies I have found have been those created by the 'big six' consulting firms. Of course those methodologies are heavily protected, as they form the intellectual property upon which they operate. They work smart, by using their intellectual property to structure the way that projects are undertaken, then after initiation they use repeatable processes to vastly reduce the time taken to produce deliverables, thereby maximizing profit. By using a clearly defined methodology, they rarely have to start from scratch.

What project managers use now

As there are very few comprehensive project management methodologies available in the market place:

● Project managers have to resort to writing their own methodology. Unfortunately because of the nature of their roles, they never have the time to research, write and implement a comprehensive methodology for their projects.
● Project managers rely on industry standard guidelines for their projects, which offer a generic framework but do not provide the depth of knowledge required to successfully undertake a project.
● Project managers are forced to initiate projects without the time to put in place a structure needed to ensure their success.

These are three real-world business problems currently experienced by project managers, business owners and consultants which have been addressed by this book. This book describes the Method123® Project Management Methodology (MPMM) by outlining the phases, activities and tasks required to undertake a project. Unlike 99 per cent of the project management books available in the market, it is not a guide to undertaking projects with useful tips, tools and techniques – this book provides an entire methodology for undertaking projects. It can be used by a student to learn how to complete a project from end-to-end, by a project manager to structure the way that a project should be undertaken and by a business owner to mandate the manner within which projects will be undertaken across the entire organization. It is a comprehensive framework that businesses can adopt, not a set of helpful hints for light reading. As such, it has been written in a clear, professional and formal manner.

The key differentiator between this methodology and those created by the 'big six' consulting firms is that this methodology is written in plain text. I have adopted industry standard terminology which can be understood by any reader with a rudimentary knowledge of project management. I have not adopted the complicated acronyms-based terminology which is prevalent throughout the industry. As such, you will not read about undertaking a PERT (project evaluation review technique) or CPA (critical path analysis), but you will read about how to create practical project plans for managing time, cost and quality within a project. This book explains the project life cycle without the fluff. It contains hundreds of practical examples, used to help managers undertake project activities quickly and efficiently.

This book stands out from the rest, because of its:

- **Depth.** Every task involved in undertaking a project is described in detail.
- **Coverage.** The methodology caters for all types of projects including IT, engineering, finance, telecommunications and government to name a few. Just as the templates based upon this methodology have been sold to a wide variety of industries, the same degree of coverage applies to this book.
- **Writing style.** Most project management books use their own terminology and are written at a level which requires at least an intermediate level of project management knowledge. This book is written in plain text without the complex terminology commonly found in the industry.
- **Tools.** A large number of tables, diagrams and checklists have been provided within this book to help readers undertake each defined activity. It is intended that for every project task listed, readers can use the knowledge acquired from this book to immediately create actual live working documents for their project.

It is intended that this book will be read by a wide variety of people in a broad spectrum of industries. The key benefits gained from reading this book are described in Table 0.1.

Table 0.1 Audience benefits

Target audience	Will benefit from
Business owners	Standardizing the manner within which projects are undertaken. Using this methodology as the basis upon which to manage the performance projects
Project managers	Having a clear framework for the successful delivery of projects. Using a comprehensive suite of processes to effectively manage time, cost, quality, change, risks, isues, suppliers and customers
Project teams	Gaining the knowledge required to build deliverables more efficiently. Not having to start from scratch, by using forms and templates
Project consultants	Being able to adopt a standard framework for managing clients projects. Using this intellectual property to rapidly build client deliverables
Trainers	Using it as a basis upon which to create training courses. Creating targeted training presentations founded on this methodology used by 45,000 people around the world
Students	Learning how to manage projects efficiently using a formal methodology. Taking their learning into the workplace, by adopting this methodology for their professional project management activities

Whether you are a manager, team member, consultant, trainer, lecturer or student, you will greatly enhance your likelihood of success by adopting the Method123® Project Management Methodology for your projects.

1

Overview

1.1 INTRODUCTION

Welcome to *The Project Management Life Cycle.* This book describes the Method123®
Project Management Methodology (MPMM) and provides a practical approach to
managing projects. Every phase, activity and task in the project life cycle is described
here in detail to help you manage staff, customers and suppliers efficiently. By reading
this book, you will gain the knowledge and confidence required to properly initiate a
project, create detailed project plans, build high-quality deliverables, monitor and
control delivery and close projects effectively. Not only will you learn how to successfully complete projects from end to end, but you will also be armed with a suite of tools
and templates to allow you to create project deliverables quickly and easily. More than
150 charts, tables and diagrams are included in this book to help explain the steps
needed to undertake a project. Each table is full of real-life examples to provide you
with the knowledge needed to complete project activities faster than before.

As there are four phases within the project life cycle, there are four chapters in this
book. Each chapter describes a particular project life cycle phase in detail, by providing
the activities and tasks required to complete the phase in its entirety. In Chapter 1 you
will learn how to initiate projects by developing a business case, undertaking a feasibility study, establishing the terms of reference, appointing the team and setting up a
project office.

Every step required to build a comprehensive suite of project plans is provided in
Chapter 2. This includes the activities required to create a project plan, resource plan,
financial plan, quality plan, risk plan, acceptance plan, communications plan and

procurement plan. The entire tender process is also defined, allowing you to create a suite of tender documentation to help you select a preferred supplier and create a supplier contract.

The most complex phase in the project life cycle (project execution) is made simple in Chapter 3 with a step-by-step guide to the nine critical management processes: time management, cost management, quality management, change management, risk management, issue management, procurement management, acceptance management and communications management.

Finally in Chapter 4, you will be shown how to formally close a project by creating a project closure report and undertaking a post implementation review. So sit back, relax and discover the vital steps needed to manage a project through the four critical phases of the project life cycle: initiation, planning, execution and closure.

1.2 WHAT IS A PROJECT?

A project is a unique endeavour to produce a set of deliverables within clearly specified time, cost and quality constraints. Projects are different from standard business operational activities as they:

- Are *unique* in nature. They do not involve repetitive processes. Every project undertaken is different from the last, whereas operational activities often involve undertaking repetitive (identical) processes.
- Have a defined *timescale*. Projects have a clearly specified start and end date within which the deliverables must be produced to meet a specified customer requirement.
- Have an approved *budget*. Projects are allocated a level of financial expenditure within which the deliverables are produced, to meet a specified customer requirement.
- Have limited *resources*. At the start of a project an agreed amount of labour, equipment and materials is allocated to the project.
- Involve an element of *risk*. Projects entail a level of uncertainty and therefore carry business risk.
- Achieve beneficial *change*. The purpose of a project is typically to improve an organization through the implementation of business change.

1.3 WHAT IS PROJECT MANAGEMENT?

Project Management is the skills, tools and management processes required to undertake a project successfully. It incorporates:

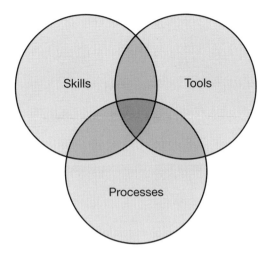

Figure 1.1 Project management components

- A set of *skills*. Specialist knowledge, skills and experience are required to reduce the level of risk within a project and thereby enhance its likelihood of success.
- A suite of *tools*. Various types of tools are used by project managers to improve their chances of success. Examples include document templates, registers, planning software, modelling software, audit checklists and review forms.
- A series of *processes*. Various processes and techniques are required to monitor and control time, cost, quality and scope on projects. Examples include time management, cost management, quality management, change management, risk management and issue management.

1.4 THE PROJECT LIFE CYCLE

Project phases

The project life cycle consists of four phases (see Figure 1.2).

Project initiation

The first phase of a project is the initiation phase. During this phase a business problem or opportunity is identified and a business case providing various solution options is defined. Next, a feasibility study is conducted to investigate whether each option addresses the business problem and a final recommended solution is then put forward. Once the recommended solution is approved, a project is initiated to deliver the approved solution. Terms of reference are completed outlining the objectives, scope

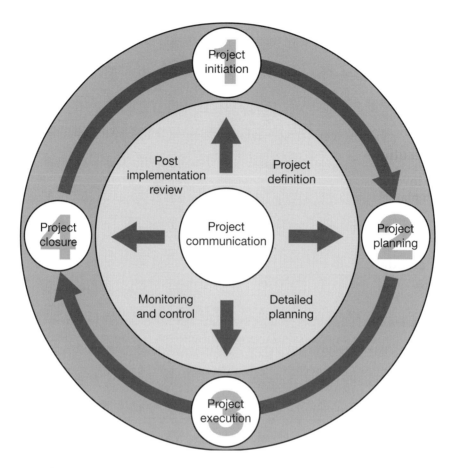

Figure 1.2   The four phases of the project life cycle

and structure of the new project, and a project manager is appointed. The project manager begins recruiting a project team and establishes a project office environment. Approval is then sought to move into the detailed planning phase.

Project planning

Once the scope of the project has been defined in the terms of reference, the project enters the detailed planning phase. This involves creating a:

- project plan outlining the activities, tasks, dependencies and timeframes;
- resource plan listing the labour, equipment and materials required;
- financial plan identifying the labour, equipment and materials costs;
- quality plan providing quality targets, assurance and control measures;

- risk plan highlighting potential risks and actions to be taken to mitigate those risks;
- acceptance plan listing the criteria to be met to gain customer acceptance;
- communications plan describing the information needed to inform stakeholders;
- procurement plan identifying products to be sourced from external suppliers.

At this point the project will have been planned in detail and is ready to be executed.

Project execution

This phase involves implementing the plans created during the project planning phase. While each plan is being executed, a series of management processes are undertaken to monitor and control the deliverables being output by the project. This includes identifying change, risks and issues, reviewing deliverable quality and measuring each deliverable produced against the acceptance criteria. Once all of the deliverables have been produced and the customer has accepted the final solution, the project is ready for closure.

Project closure

Project closure involves releasing the final deliverables to the customer, handing over project documentation to the business, terminating supplier contracts, releasing project resources and communicating the closure of the project to all stakeholders. The last remaining step is to undertake a post-implementation review to quantify the level of project success and identify any lessons learnt for future projects.

Now that you have an overall appreciation of the project life cycle, I will explain each life cycle phase in the following sections.

Project initiation

Within the initiation phase, the business problem or opportunity is identified, a solution is defined, a project is formed and a project team is appointed to build and deliver the solution to the customer. Figure 1.3 shows the activities undertaken during the initiation phase:

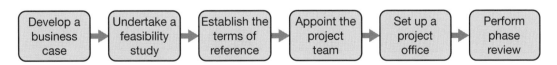

Figure 1.3   Project initiation activities

Develop a business case

The trigger to initiating a project is identifying a business problem or opportunity to be addressed. A business case is created to define the problem or opportunity in detail and identify a preferred solution for implementation. The business case includes:

- a detailed description of the problem or opportunity;
- a list of the alternative solutions available;
- an analysis of the business benefits, costs, risks and issues;
- a description of the preferred solution;
- a summarized plan for implementation.

The business case is then approved by an identified project sponsor, and the required funding is allocated to proceed with a feasibility study.

Undertake a feasibility study

At any stage during or after the creation of a business case, a formal feasibility study may be commissioned. The purpose of a feasibility study is to assess the likelihood of each alternative solution option achieving the benefits outlined in the business case. The feasibility study will also investigate whether the forecast costs are reasonable, the solution is achievable, the risks are acceptable and the identified issues are avoidable.

Establish the terms of reference

After the business case and feasibility study have been approved, a new project is formed. At this point, terms of reference are created. The terms of reference define the vision, objectives, scope and deliverables for the new project. They also describe the organization structure, activities, resources and funding required to undertake the project. Any risks, issues, planning assumptions and constraints are also identified.

Appoint the project team

The project team are now ready to be appointed. Although a project manager may be appointed at any stage during the life of the project, the manager will ideally be appointed prior to recruiting the project team. The project manager creates a detailed job description for each role in the project team, and recruits people into each role based on their relevant skills and experience.

Set up a project office

The project office is the physical environment within which the team is based. Although it is usual to have one central project office, it is possible to have a virtual project office with project team members located around the world. A project office environment should include:

- equipment, such as office furniture, computer equipment, stationery and materials;
- communications infrastructure, such as telephones, computer network, e-mail, Internet access, file storage, database storage and backup facilities;
- documentation, such as a project methodology, standards, processes, forms and registers;
- tools, such as accounting, project planning and risk modelling software.

Perform a phase review

At the end of the initiation phase, a phase review is performed. This is basically a checkpoint to ensure that the project has achieved its objectives as planned.

Project planning

By now, the project costs and benefits have been documented, the objectives and scope have been defined, the project team has been appointed and a formal project office environment established. It is now time to undertake detailed planning to ensure that the activities performed during the execution phase of the project are properly sequenced, resourced, executed and controlled. The activities shown in Figure 1.4 are undertaken.

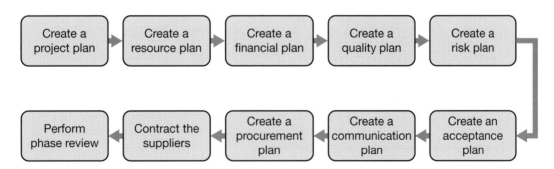

Figure 1.4 Project planning activities

Create a project plan

The first step in the project planning phase is to document the project plan. A 'work breakdown structure' (WBS) is identified which includes a hierarchical set of phases, activities and tasks to be undertaken to complete the project. After the WBS has been agreed, an assessment of the level of effort required to undertake each activity and task is made. The activities and tasks are then sequenced, resources are allocated and a detailed project schedule is formed. This project plan is the key tool used by the project manager to assess the progress of the project throughout the project life cycle.

Create a resource plan

Immediately after the project plan is formed, the level of resource required to under-take each of the activities and tasks listed within the project plan will need to be allo-cated. Although generic resource may have already been allocated in the project plan, a detailed resource plan is required to identify the:

- type of resource required, such as labour, equipment and materials;
- quantity of each type of resource required;
- roles, responsibilities and skill-sets of all *human* resource required;
- specifications of all *equipment* resource required;
- items and quantities of *material* resource required.

A schedule is assembled for each type of resource so that the project manager can review the resource allocation at each stage in the project.

Create a financial plan

A financial plan is created to identify the total quantity of money required to undertake each phase in the project (in other words, the budget). The total cost of labour, equip-ment and materials is calculated and an expense schedule is defined which enables the project manager to measure the forecast spend versus the actual spend throughout the project. Detailed financial planning is an extremely important activity within the project, as the customer will expect the final solution to have been delivered within the allocated budget.

Create a quality plan

Meeting the quality expectations of the customer can be a challenging task. To ensure that the quality expectations are clearly defined and can reasonably be achieved, a quality plan is documented. The quality plan:

- Defines the term 'quality' for the project.
- Lists clear and unambiguous quality targets for each deliverable. Each quality target provides a set of criteria and standards to be achieved to meet the expectations of the customer.
- Provides a plan of activities to assure the customer that the quality targets will be met (in other words, a quality assurance plan).
- Identifies the techniques used to control the actual quality level of each deliverable as it is built (in other words, a quality control plan).

Not only is it important to review the quality of the deliverables produced by the project, it is also important to review the quality of the management processes which produced them. A quality plan will summarize each of the management processes undertaken during the project, including time, cost, quality, change, risk, issue, procurement, acceptance and communications management.

Create a risk plan

The next step is to document all foreseeable project risks within a risk plan. This plan also identifies the actions required to prevent each risk from occurring, as well as reduce the impact of the risk should it eventuate. Developing a clear risk plan is an important activity within the planning phase, as it is necessary to mitigate all critical project risks prior to entering the execution phase of the project.

Create an acceptance plan

To deliver the project successfully, you will need to gain full acceptance from the customer that the deliverables produced by the project meet or exceed requirements. An acceptance plan is created to help achieve this, by clarifying the completion criteria for each deliverable and providing a schedule of acceptance reviews. These reviews provide the customer with the opportunity to assess each deliverable and provide formal acceptance that it meets the requirements as originally stated.

Create a communications plan

Prior to the execution phase, it is also necessary to identify how each of the stakeholders will be kept informed of the progress of the project. The communications plan identifies the types of information to be distributed to stakeholders, the methods of distributing the information, the frequency of distribution, and responsibilities of each person in the project team for distributing the information.

Create a procurement plan

The last planning activity within the planning phase is to identify the elements of the project to be acquired from external suppliers. The procurement plan provides a detailed description of the products (that is, goods and services) to be acquired from suppliers, the justification for acquiring each product externally as opposed to from within the business, and the schedule for product delivery. It also describes the process for the selection of a preferred supplier (the tender process), and the ordering and delivery of the products (the procurement process).

Contract the suppliers

Although external suppliers may be appointed at any stage of the project, it is usual to appoint suppliers after the project plans have been documented but prior to the execution phase of the project. Only at this point will the project manager have a clear idea of the role of suppliers and the expectations for their delivery. A formal tender process is undertaken to identify a short-list of capable suppliers and select a preferred supplier to initiate contractual discussions with. The tender process involves creating a statement of work, a request for information and request for proposal document to obtain sufficient information from each potential supplier and select the preferred supplier. Once a preferred supplier has been chosen, a contract is agreed between the project team and the supplier for the delivery of the requisite products.

Perform a phase review

At the end of the planning phase, a phase review is performed. This is a checkpoint to ensure that the project has achieved its objectives as planned.

Project execution

The execution phase is typically the longest phase of the project in terms of duration. It is the phase within which the deliverables are physically constructed and presented to the customer for acceptance. To ensure that the customer's requirements are met, the project manager monitors and controls the activities, resources and expenditure required to build each deliverable. A number of management processes are undertaken to ensure that the project proceeds as planned. The activities shown in Figure 1.5 are undertaken.

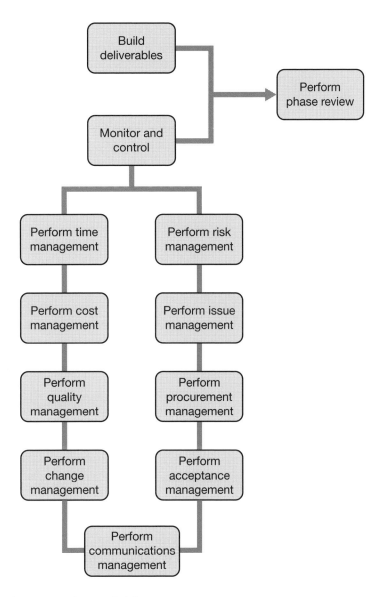

Figure 1.5 Project execution activities

Build the deliverables

This phase involves physically constructing each deliverable for acceptance by the customer. The activities undertaken to construct each deliverable will vary depending on the type of project being undertaken. Activities may be undertaken in a 'waterfall' fashion, where each activity is completed in sequence until the final deliverable is produced, or an 'iterative' fashion, where iterations of each deliverable are constructed until the deliverable meets the requirements of the customer. Regardless of the method used to construct each deliverable, careful monitoring and control processes should be employed to ensure that the quality of the final deliverable meets the acceptance criteria set by the customer.

Monitor and control

While the project team are physically producing each deliverable, the project manager implements a series of management processes to monitor and control the activities being undertaken by the project team. An overview of each management process follows.

Time Management

Time management is the process of recording and controlling time spent by staff on the project. As time is a scarce resource within projects, each team member should record time spent undertaking project activities on a timesheet form. This will enable the project manager to control the amount of time spent undertaking each activity within the project. A timesheet register is also completed, providing a summary of the time spent on the project in total so that the project plan can always be kept fully up to date.

Cost management

Cost management is the process by which costs/expenses incurred on the project are formally identified, approved and paid. Expense forms are completed for each set of related project expenses such as labour, equipment and materials costs. Expense forms are approved by the project manager and recorded within an expense register for auditing purposes.

Quality management

Quality is defined as the extent to which the final deliverable conforms to the customer requirements. Quality management is the process by which quality is assured and controlled for the project, using quality assurance and quality control techniques. Quality reviews are undertaken frequently and the results recorded on a quality review form.

Change management

Change management is the process by which changes to the project scope, deliverables, timescales or resources are formally requested, evaluated and approved prior to implementation. A core aspect of the project manager's role is to manage change within the project. This is achieved by understanding the business and system drivers requiring the change, identifying the costs and benefits of adopting the change, and formulating a structured plan for implementing the change. To formally request a change to the project, a change form is completed. The status of all active change forms should be recorded within a change register.

Risk management

Risk management is the process by which risks to the project are formally identified, quantified and managed. A project risk may be identified at any stage of the project by completing a risk form and recording the relevant risk details within the risk register.

Issue management

Issue management is the method by which issues currently affecting the ability of the project to produce the required deliverable are formally managed. After an issue form has been completed and the details logged in the issue register, each issue is evaluated by the project manager and a set of actions undertaken to resolve the issue identified.

Procurement management

Procurement management is the process of sourcing products from an external supplier. Purchase orders are used to purchase products from suppliers, and a procurement register is maintained to track each purchase request through to its completion.

Acceptance management

Acceptance management is the process of gaining customer acceptance for deliverables produced by the project. Acceptance forms are used to enable project staff to request acceptance for a deliverable, once complete. Each acceptance form identifies the acceptance criteria, review methods and results of the acceptance reviews undertaken.

Communications management

Communications management is the process by which formal communications messages are identified, created, reviewed and communicated within a project. The most common method of communicating the status of the project is via a project status report. Each communications message released is captured in a communications register.

Perform a phase review

At the end of the execution phase, a phase review is performed. This is a checkpoint to ensure that the project has achieved its objectives as planned.

Project closure

Following the acceptance of all project deliverables by the customer, the project will have met its objectives and be ready for closure. Project closure is the last phase in the project life cycle, and must be conducted formally so that the business benefits delivered by the project are fully realized by the customer. The activities outlined in Figure 1.6 are undertaken.

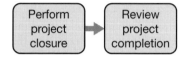

Figure 1.6   Project closure activities

Perform project closure

Project closure, or 'close-out', essentially involves winding up the project. This includes:

● determining whether all of the project completion criteria have been met;
● identifying any outstanding project activities, risks or issues;
● handing over all project deliverables and documentation to the customer;
● cancelling supplier contracts and releasing project resources to the business;
● communicating the closure of the project to all stakeholders and interested parties.

A project closure report is documented and submitted to the customer and/or project sponsor for approval. The project manager is responsible for undertaking each of the activities identified in the project closure report, and the project is closed only when all the activities listed in the project closure report have been completed.

Review project completion

The final activity within a project is the review of its success by an independent party. Success is determined by how well it performed against the defined objectives and conformed to the management processes outlined in the planning phase. To determine how well it performed, the following types of questions are answered:

● Did it result in the benefits defined in the business case?
● Did it achieve the objectives outlined in the terms of reference?
● Did it operate within the scope of the terms of reference?
● Did the deliverables meet the criteria defined in the quality plan?

- Was it delivered within the schedule outlined in the project plan?
- Was it delivered within the budget outlined in the financial plan?

To determine how well it conformed, an assessment is made of the level of conformity to the management processes outlined in the quality plan. These results, as well as a list of the key achievements and lessons learnt, are documented within a post-implementation review and presented to the customer and/or project sponsor for approval.

This completes the project life cycle overview. I hope that by now you will have a strong appreciation of the steps involved in undertaking a project. We will now explore the project initiation, planning, execution and closure phases in depth, providing you with all of the knowledge required to successfully complete your project.

2

Project initiation

2.1 INTRODUCTION

The first phase in the project life cycle is project initiation. This phase involves creating a new project by defining the business problem or opportunity to be addressed, the solution to be delivered and the scope within which the project will be undertaken. The activities outlined in Figure 2.1 need to be completed.

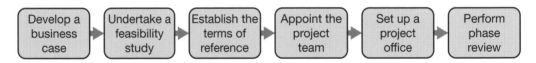

Figure 2.1   Project initiation activities

Although it might not be evident, the project initiation phase is by far the most critical phase in the project life cycle. If you do not properly initiate the project, you will greatly increase the risk of project failure. It takes time, diligence and patience to ensure that the project is properly defined and scoped before it is executed. Unfortunately a large number of projects quickly pass through this phase by:

● failing to properly define the business benefits and costs associated with the project;
● assuming that the solution identified is feasible, without conducting feasibility testing;

- defining the *generic* objectives, scope and deliverables of the project, without any sound basis for measuring performance.

This is the reason that many projects suffer from scope creep, late delivery and excess spending. To avoid these common pitfalls, you need to complete each step listed here as thoroughly as possible. If you achieve this, you can feel confident that your project has a solid foundation for success. The following sections define in detail the steps required to successfully initiate a project.

2.2 DEVELOP A BUSINESS CASE

The first step you need to take to initiate a project is to develop a business case. A business case is a document which justifies the start-up of a project. It includes:

- a description of the problem or opportunity that exists in the business;
- a list of the available options for delivering a solution to resolve the problem;
- a list of the costs and benefits associated with each solution option;
- a recommended solution option for approval.

The business case is usually presented by senior management in the business to an identified business sponsor or customer. During the creation of a business case, it may be necessary to undertake a feasibility study. This process involves undertaking a more detailed assessment of the current business problem or opportunity, the various solution options available and the likelihood of each alternative solution meeting the customer's requirements. The feasibility study adds more rigour to the solution options defined in the business case.

   The business case is referred to throughout the project to determine whether the costs, benefits, risks and issues align with those originally documented. At the end of the project, a post-implementation review (PIR) will be undertaken to determine whether the project delivered the business benefits outlined in the business case. In this regard, the success of the project is measured against the ability of the project to meet the criteria outlined in the business case.

Identify the business problem

Perform an environmental analysis

To create a business case, start by identifying the core aspects of the business environment which resulted in the need for this project to take place. Examples include:

- changes to the business vision, strategy or objectives;
- particular business processes or technologies that are not operating efficiently;

- new competitor products or processes which have been identified;
- opportunities resulting from new technologies introduced to the market place;
- commercial or operational trends which are driving changes in the business;
- changes to statutory, legislative or other environmental requirements.

You should collate any evidence to support the conclusions drawn above.

Complete a problem analysis

Then describe the business problem or opportunity to be addressed by the project. Write a summary of the core business problem, including:

- a full description of the problem;
- the reasons the problem exists;
- the elements that create the problem (such as human, process, and technology factors);
- the impact the problem is having on the business (such as financial, cultural or operational impact);
- the timeframes within which the problem must be resolved.

Write a summary of the core business opportunity, including:

- a full description of the opportunity;
- any supporting evidence to prove that the opportunity is real;
- the timeframe within which the opportunity will exist;
- the impact that realization of the opportunity will have on the business.

Assess the available options

After defining the business problem or opportunity, list all of the alternative solution options, their benefits, costs, feasibility, risks and issues. Try to minimize the number of options available by conducting a detailed feasibility study. Complete the following steps.

Identify the options

Identify each of the alternative solutions and create a detailed description for each.

Quantify the benefits

Identify the financial and non-financial business benefits to be gained from implementing each alternative solution, by completing Table 2.1.

Table 2.1   Business benefits

Benefit category	Benefit description	Benefit value
Financial	New revenue generated Reduction in costs Increased profit margin	\$ x \$ x \$ x
Operational	Improved operational efficiency Reduction in product time to market Enhanced quality of product/service	x % x hours x %
Market	Increased market awareness Greater market share Additional competitive advantage	x % x % Describe
Customer	Improved customer satisfaction Increased customer retention Greater customer loyalty	x % x % Describe
Staff	Increased staff organizational culture Longer staff retention	Describe x %
...	...	...

Collate any supporting materials, such as statistical analysis and historical trend analysis, to support the benefits listed above.

Forecast the costs

Identify the business expenses involved with implementing each alternative solution, by completing Table 2.2.

Note that you may need to identify whether the expense item is a capital expense (CAPEX) or operational expense (OPEX). A separate spreadsheet providing an analysis of each of the expenses may need to be provided.

Table 2.2 Business costs

Expense category	Expense description	Expense value	Expense type
People	Salaries of project staff Contractors/outsourced parties Training courses	$ x $ x $ x	OPEX CAPEX OPEX
Physical	Building premises for project team Equipment and materials Tools (computers, phones etc)	$ x $ x $ x	OPEX OPEX OPEX
Marketing	Advertising/branding Promotional materials PR and communications	$ x $ x $ x	CAPEX CAPEX CAPEX
Organizational	Operational down-time Short-term loss in productivity Cultural change	$ x $ x Describe	OPEX OPEX n/a
...	...	...	...

Assess the feasibility

Assess the overall feasibility of each solution option. A feasibility study may need to be undertaken to identify the likelihood of each solution satisfying the business problem or opportunity. Complete Table 2.3 for each alternative solution.

In the example provided, the likelihood of new technology delivering the required result is very high, as it has been rated 9 out of 10. To come to this conclusion, a technology prototype was created.

Table 2.3 Solution feasibility

Solution component	Feasibility rating (1–10)	Method used to determine feasibility
New technology	9	A technology prototype was created to assess the solution
New people	8	A survey was completed to identify skill-set availability
New processes	3	Processes within similar organizations were reviewed
New assets	9	Physical assets were inspected
...	...	...

Identify any risks

Risks are defined as any event that may adversely affect the ability of the solution to produce the required deliverables. Summarize the most apparent risks associated with the adoption of each solution. For each risk, identify the mitigating actions required to reduce the likelihood of it occurring, as well as reduce the impact on the project should the risk actually eventuate. Complete Table 2.4 for each alternative solution.

Table 2.4   Business risks

Risk description	Risk likelihood	Risk impact	Actions required to mitigate risk
Inability to recruit skilled resource	Low	Very high	Outsource project to a company with proven industry experience and skilled staff
Technology solution is unable to deliver required results	Medium	High	Complete a pilot project to prove the technology solution will deliver the required results
Additional capital expenditure may be required	Medium	Medium	Maintain strict cost management processes during the project
...	...	...	...

To complete this section thoroughly, it may be necessary to complete a risk management plan.

Document the issues

Summarize the highest priority issues associated with the adoption of each solution. Issues are defined as any event that currently adversely affects the ability of the solution to produce the required deliverables. Complete Table 2.5 for each alternative solution:

Table 2.5 Business issues

Issue description	Issue priority	Action required to resolve issue
Required capital expenditure funds have not been budgeted	High	Request funding approval as part of this proposal
Required computer software is only at beta phase and has not yet been released live	Medium	Design solution based on current software version and adapt changes to solution once the final version of the software has been released
Regulatory approval must be sought to implement the final solution	Low	Initiate the regulatory approval process early so that it does not delay the final roll-out process
...	...	...

List any assumptions

List any assumptions associated with the adoption of each alternative solution. Examples include:

- There will be no legislative, business strategy or policy changes during the project.
- Prices of raw materials will not increase during the course of the project.
- Additional resource will be available from the business as required.

Recommend a preferred solution

You should now compare each of the alternative solutions and recommend a preferred solution for implementation.

Rank the alternative solutions

Identify the assessment criteria required to compare each of the alternative solutions and then agree a mechanism for rating the solutions to determine an overall score. Although a simple rating mechanism (such as applying a score from 1 to 10) may be used, you may wish to weight criteria which are important to the final decision. Use Table 2.6 to help you summarize the ratings given to each alternative solution.

Table 2.6 Solution ranking

Assessment criteria	Solution 1 rating	Solution 2 rating	Solution 3 rating
Benefits • Increased revenue • Reduced expenditure • Improved efficiency • Enhanced quality • Other	(1–10 rating)	(1–10 rating)	(1–10 rating)
Costs • People • Physical • Marketing • Organizational • Other			
Feasibility • Technology components • People components • Process components • Asset components • Other			
Risks • Resource • Technology • Organizational • Other			
Total score			
...	...	...	...

Identify the recommended solution

The solution option with the highest total score in Table 2.6 will become your preferred solution. This solution will be explicitly listed in your business case document along with the primary reasons that this solution was chosen over the other potential solutions identified.

Describe the implementation approach

The final activity involved in creating a business case is to provide the project sponsors with confidence that the implementation of the preferred solution has been well thought through. To do this, describe in detail how the project will be initiated, planned, executed and closed as follows.

Project initiation

List the steps involved in defining the project, recruiting the project team and establishing the project office.

Project planning

Describe the overall planning process to show that the project phases, activities and tasks will be undertaken in a coordinated fashion.

Project execution

List the activities required to build the deliverables that create the solution for the customer.

Project closure

List the activities involved with handing over the final solution to the customer, releasing staff, closing the project office and performing a post-implementation review of the project.

Project management

Describe in brief how the following aspects of the project will be undertaken:

- time management;
- cost management;
- quality management;
- change management;
- risk management;
- issue management;
- procurement management;
- communications management;
- acceptance management.

You are now ready to collate all of the materials listed in this section and create your business case document for approval.

2.3 UNDERTAKE A FEASIBILITY STUDY

A feasibility study involves undertaking a detailed assessment of a current business problem or opportunity, identifying the various solution options available and determining the likelihood of each alternative solution meeting a customer's requirements. The outcome of the exercise is the creation of a feasibility study document which provides:

- a full description of the business problem;
- a list of the requirements for a solution to fix the problem;
- a list of all available options for delivering a solution;
- an assessment of the feasibility of each option;
- a list of the risks and issues associated with each option;
- the preferred solution option for implementation.

The feasibility study document is presented by senior management in the business to the business sponsor or customer. Although a feasibility study may be conducted prior to the completion of a business case, it is usually undertaken as part of the overall business case process to add more rigour to the solution options presented. For this reason, the topics covered in the business case and feasibility study documents are similar.

Note that a feasibility study may be undertaken to address a *business problem* to be resolved, or a *business opportunity* to be realized. Although this section refers primarily to the resolution of business problems, each section equally applies to the realization of business opportunities.

Investigate the business problem

Research the business environment

Before you undertake a feasibility study, you should first have a full appreciation of the business problem to be addressed. To achieve this, first research the business environment within which the problem is contained.

External analysis

Identify the external environment within which the business operates by defining the market segment, competition and relevant products and services available. Also identify the market, technology and commercial trends, as well as any statutory or legislative changes.

Business vision

Identify the business vision, strategy and objectives for the short, medium and long term.

Business units

List each of the current business units (such as the finance department) relevant to this project. Show them in an organization chart, highlighting the internal reporting and communication lines.

Business locations

Identify the geographic location of each business unit identified. If necessary, show each business location on a geographical map to highlight the physical placement of business units in relation to one another.

Business information

Identify the major types of business information relevant to the project such as financial, human resources and asset-related information. List the repositories holding this information such as financial databases, human resources directories and asset systems. If appropriate, create a data flow diagram to show how information is used within the business to undertake relevant business processes.

Business technologies

List each of the technologies relevant to the project and describe their business functions. Where suitable, describe the make-up of each technology in a technology architecture diagram, highlighting the interfaces for each technology.

Business processes

List each of the current business processes relevant to the project and provide a detailed description for each. Show all business processes on a process flow diagram to describe the flow and interaction between each business process listed.

Research the business problem

Business problem

Identify the core business problem to be addressed. In particular, note the reasons the problem exists, the impact it is having on the business and the timeframe in which it must be resolved. Examples of typical business problems include those related to:

- Business process:
  - efficiency, timeliness, ownership;
  - clarity, accuracy, relevancy.

- Business unit:
  - definition (eg lack of vision, scope, objectives);
  - direction (eg lack of alignment with corporate vision);
  - structure (eg inefficient/inappropriate structure);
  - size (eg too small or large);
  - makeup (eg lack of skills, experience);
  - performance (eg inadequate product/service quality);
  - data (eg poor data quality).
- Business location:
  - security (eg security exposures or risks);
  - relevancy (eg location does not fit with corporate image);
  - finances (eg location is too expensive);
  - physical appearance (eg deterioration).
- Business technology:
  - reliability, scalability, and performance;
  - relevancy (any misfit between technology and business objectives).

Business opportunity

List any business opportunities identified. In particular, note any supporting evidence to confirm that an opportunity currently exists, the time for which the opportunity will remain and the impact that realizing the opportunity will have on the business. Examples of typical business opportunities include:

- new market demand identified;
- competitor company failure or change;
- new ideas for products or services;
- new business premises made available;
- new technologies available for usage;
- new skill-sets available in market;
- changes in legislation or regulatory requirements.

Identify the requirements

List the key business drivers

List the key business drivers for this project. Examples include:

- a particular business objective which must be achieved within a certain period;
- changes to legislation/regulation which come into effect on a certain date;
- a limited timeframe for competitive advantage;
- timing of other related changes in the business or external market place.

Define the business requirements

For each business problem or opportunity, list the requirements for a solution. For example, you may need:

- a new process to be implemented which improves business efficiency;
- to establish a new business unit to deliver a new product to market;
- to build new physical premises which provides more capacity.

Complete Table 2.7.

Table 2.7 Business requirements

Business problem/opportunity	Project requirement
Description	Description
...	...

Undertake a feasibility study

Now that you have identified the business environment, drivers, problem and requirements, you are ready to undertake the feasibility study. This section describes how to complete the feasibility study by identifying each of the potential solutions and determining the likelihood of each alternative solution meeting the requirements of the customer. It also describes the risks, issues and assumptions associated with each alternative solution.

Identify the potential solutions

Create a full list of potential solutions to the business problem or opportunity. For each potential solution, list its components and describe its purpose. Also consider how each particular component addresses the key business requirements identified above.

Undertake the assessment

Assess the actual feasibility of each alternative solution using a range of assessment methods. Examples of assessment methods include:

- **Prototyping.** A prototype is a subset of the full solution which is constructed to prove that at least part of the full solution is achievable. Prototypes are typically developed to prove that the highest risk areas of the solution are feasible. For instance, if the solution was to involve the implementation of a new computer system, a prototype might be built to test that the system could be integrated with other systems used in the business.

- **Staff surveys.** Staff surveys are a great technique for identifying the feasibility of solutions that involve a change to business processes. For instance, they may be used to identify the likely adoption of a new performance management process by staff.
- **Market surveys.** Market surveys may be undertaken to assess the feasibility of introducing new products or services to the market by determining the level of potential customer demand.

Note: In some cases it may not be practical to undertake formal methods for the assessment of feasibility. Careful consideration and a 'best guess' may be the only methods available.

Measure the results

Measure the overall result of each assessment by scoring the actual versus expected result and listing other non-tangible considerations that also need to be taken into account in the final rankings.

Identify any risks

List the apparent risks associated with the implementation of each solution. Risks are defined as any event that may adversely affect the ability of the solution to produce the required deliverables. Risks may be strategic, environmental, financial, operational, technical, competitor or customer-related. Document the risks by completing Table 2.8.

Table 2.8 Solution risks

Risk description	Risk likelihood	Risk impact	Actions required to mitigate risk
Inability to recruit skilled resource	Low	Very high	Outsource project to a company with proven industry experience and appropriately skilled staff
Technology solution is unable to deliver required results	Medium	High	Complete a pilot project to prove the full technology solution
Additional capital expenditure may be required in addition to that approved	Medium	Medium	Maintain strict capital expenditure processes during the project
...	...	...	...

Prioritize the issues

Identify any issues associated with the adoption of each solution. Issues are defined as any event that currently adversely affects the ability of the solution to produce the required deliverables. Document the issues by completing Table 2.9.

Table 2.9 Solution issues

Issue description	Issue priority	Actions required to resolve issue
Required capital expenditure funds have not been budgeted	High	Request funding approval as part of this proposal
Required computer software is only at beta phase and has not yet been released live	Medium	Design solution based on current software version and adapt changes to solution once the final version of the software has been released
Council approval must be sought to implement the final solution	Low	Initiate the council approval process early so that it does not delay the final roll-out process
...	...	...

List any assumptions

List any assumptions associated with the adoption of each solution. For example:

- There will be no legislative, business strategy or policy changes during this project.
- Prices of raw materials will not increase during the course of the project.
- Additional human resources will be available from the business to support the project.

Rank the feasibility results

Define the criteria

Specify the criteria used to rank each of the solution options and describe the scoring and weighting mechanism used to produce an overall result.

Assign ranking scores

Score each option against the identified criteria, using Table 2.10.

Table 2.10 Solution feasibility

Criterion	Option 1 Score	Weight Total	Option 2 Score	Weight Total	Option 3 Score	Weight Total
Criterion 1						
Criterion 2						
Criterion 3						
Criterion 4						
Criterion 5						
Criterion 6						
Criterion 7						
Criterion 8						
Criterion 9						
Criterion 10						
Total score						

Note that a score is typically a number from 1 (low feasibility) to 10 (high feasibility), and a weight is a number from 0.5 (criterion is unimportant) to 1.5 (criterion is very important). The total is calculated as score multiplied by weight.

Identify the feasibility outcome

Based on the total score, identify the most feasible option to be recommended for implementation.

You are now ready to collate all of the materials listed in this section and create your feasibility study document for approval. The next step in the project life cycle is to define the terms of reference.

2.4 ESTABLISH THE TERMS OF REFERENCE

Now that you have documented a business case and undertaken a feasibility study to select your preferred solution, you are ready to define the scope of a project to deliver the solution to your customer. To formally define the scope of a project, you need to document its terms of reference (TOR).

The TOR outlines the purpose of the project, the way it will be structured and how it will be implemented. It describes the project:

- vision, objectives, scope and deliverables (ie what you have to achieve);
- stakeholders, roles and responsibilities (ie who will take part in it);
- resource, financial and quality plans (ie how it will be undertaken).

The TOR may also be referred to as a 'project charter' or 'project definition report'. It is usually presented by senior management in the business to the business sponsor or customer for approval. It is completed after the business case and feasibility study have been approved but before the project team is appointed. The TOR also defines the scope of the project, within which all deliverables are produced. Project activities will only be undertaken outside the defined scope of the project if a valid change request form has been approved.

Identify the project vision

To establish a TOR, you first need to formally define the purpose of project. This includes the vision for the project, the key objectives to be met, the scope of work to be undertaken and the deliverables to be produced.

Vision

Describe the overall vision of the project. The vision statement should be short, concise and achievable. Examples of vision statements include:

- To deliver a robust, scalable financial management system to the business.
- To procure new work premises with adequate capacity for 500 people.
- To successfully introduce new customer service processes to the business.

Objectives

List the key objectives of the project. Objectives are statements which describe in more detail what it is that the project will achieve. All objectives listed should be specific, measurable, achievable, realistic and time-bound (SMART). Examples include:

- To deliver new accounts payable and receivable and payroll processes, thereby reducing financial processing timescales by at least 30 per cent.
- To build new work premises with 50 per cent more space, 30 per cent more car parks and 20 per cent fewer operational costs than the existing premises.
- To provide a new customer complaints service to enable customers to issue complaints online and receive a direct response from the company within 24 hours.
- To install a new accounts payable, receivable and payroll system, resulting in a 20 per cent improvement in accounting efficiencies.
- To relocate existing technology infrastructure at the new building premises within a two-month timeframe with no impact on customer service delivery.
- To build a new website which allows customers to track customer complaints.

Scope

Define the formal scope of the project, including the business products, services, processes, departments, data and technologies affected. Where relevant, identify any business areas not affected by this project to further clarify the project scope boundaries.

Deliverables

Highlight the key project deliverables using Table 2.11.

Table 2.11   Project deliverables

Deliverable	Components	Description
New physical premises	New physical building	1,200 sq m premises near city centre with outdoor facilities, parking and signage
	Interior fit-out	Open plan environment with 5 offices, 3 meeting rooms and a staff games room
	Telecommunications	Voice / data telecoms infrastructure and video conference facilities
New financial system	Accounts payable module	A new system module which enables staff to quickly enter accounts payable transactions
	Accounts receivable module	A new system module which enables staff to quickly enter accounts receivable transactions
	Payroll module	A new system module which enables staff to quickly enter payroll information
New customer complaints process	Complaints website	New website with customer complaints forms, a complaint tracking page and company contact information
	Complaints resolution process	New full-time staff complaints role and process for resolving complaints made
	Complaints measurement process	New process for assessing complaint characteristics (such as numbers, business areas and resolution timescales)
...	...	...

Describe the project organization

Customers

List the customers who intend to use the deliverables produced by the project. Customers may be individuals or groups within or outside the company. The success of the project will be based primarily on whether or not the deliverables produced match the requirements of the customers identified in Table 2.12.

Table 2.12   Project organization

Customer	Representative
Customer group	Customer name
...	...

Stakeholders

List the stakeholders for this project. A 'stakeholder' is simply a person or entity outside the project that has a key interest or 'stake' in the project. For instance, a company financial controller will have an interest in the cost implications of the project, and a CEO will have an interest in whether the project helps to achieve the vision of the company. Other examples of stakeholders include company executives, legislative bodies and regulatory bodies. Complete Table 2.13.

Table 2.13   Project stakeholders

Stakeholder	Stakeholder interest
CEO	Alignment with company vision
Financial controller	Alignment with company budget
Health and safety office	Alignment with health and safety standards
Government body	Compliance with legislation
Industry body	Compliance with codes of practice
...	...

Roles

Identify the roles required to undertake the project. Typical roles include a project sponsor, project manager, review group and team member. For each role, list the name of the person likely to fill the role, the organization, the assignment status and the date the person is to be assigned to the project if he or she has not already been assigned. Complete Table 2.14.

Table 2.14   Project roles

Role	Resource name	Organization	Assignment status	Assignment date
Role	Person	Organization	Unasigned / assigned	xx / yy / zz
...	...	...	...	...

For larger projects with more than 10 staff, list only the key roles in the above table. Include a detailed listing and description of all roles in a separate resource plan if required.

Responsibilities

Now that it is clear which roles are required to undertake the project, you are ready to describe the primary responsibilities of each role. You only need to provide a summarized list of responsibilities at this stage, as a full set of responsibilities will be documented in a separate job description for each role later in the life cycle. Examples of typical project roles and responsibilities have been provided below.

Project sponsor

The project sponsor is the principal 'owner' of the project. Responsibilities include:

- defining the vision and high-level objectives for the project;
- approving the requirements, timetable, resources and budget;
- authorizing the provision of funds / resources (internal or external);
- approving the project plan and quality plan;
- ensuring that major business risks are identified and managed;
- approving any major changes in scope;
- receiving project review group minutes and taking action accordingly;
- resolving issues escalated by the project manager / project review group;
- ensuring the participation of all business resource, where required;
- providing final acceptance of the solution upon project completion.

Project review group

The project review group may include both business and third-party representatives, and is put in place to ensure that the project progresses according to plan. Responsibilities include:

- assisting the project sponsor with the definition of the project vision and objectives;
- undertaking quality reviews prior to the completion of each project milestone;
- ensuring that all business risks are identified and managed accordingly;
- ensuring conformance to the standards and processes identified in the quality plan;
- ensuring that appropriate client/vendor contractual documentation is established.

Project manager

The project manager ensures that the daily activities undertaken on the project are in accordance with the approved project plans. The project manager is responsible for ensuring that the project produces the required deliverables on time, within budgeted cost and to the level of quality outlined within the quality plan. Responsibilities include:

- documenting the detailed project plan and quality plan;
- ensuring that all required resources are assigned to the project and clearly tasked;
- managing assigned resources according to the defined scope of the project;
- implementing the project processes (time/cost/quality/change/risk/issue/procurement/communication/acceptance management);
- monitoring and reporting project performance (schedule, cost, quality and risk);
- ensuring compliance with the processes and standards outlined in the quality plan;
- adjusting the project plan to monitor and control the progress of the project;
- reporting and escalating project risks and issues;
- managing project interdependencies.

Project team member

Each project team member undertakes the tasks necessary to design, build and implement the final solution. Responsibilities include:

- completing tasks allocated by the project manager;
- reporting progress to the project manager on a frequent basis;
- maintaining documentation relating to the execution of allocated tasks;
- escalating risks and issues to be addressed by the project manager.

Structure

Show the reporting lines between each of the key roles on a project organization chart. An example is given in Figure 2.2.

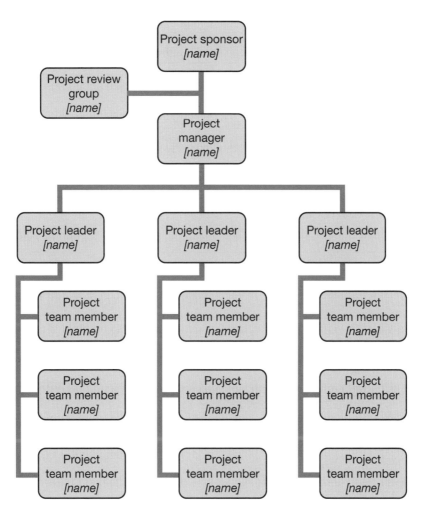

Figure 2.2   Project organization chart

Build a generic project plan

Project approach

Describe the overall approach to initiating, planning, executing and closing the project using Table 2.15.

Table 2.15 Project approach

Phase	Overall approach
Initiation	Outline the method by which the project will be further defined, the project team appointed and the project office established
Planning	Define the overall planning process to ensure that the phases, activities and tasks are undertaken in a coordinated fashion
Execution	Describe the generic phases and activities required to build, test and implement the deliverables of the project
Closure	Describe the steps required to release the deliverables to the business, close the project office, reallocate staff and perform a post-implementation review (PIR) of the project
...	...

Project plan

Create a summarized plan listing the phases, activities and timeframes in the project. (See Figure 2.3 for an example.)

Next, list the major project milestones and explain why each milestone is critical to the project, as in Table 2.16. A milestone is an important event within the project, such as the achievement of a key project deliverable or a business/external event impacting the project.

Table 2.16 Project milestones

Milestone	Date	Description
Milestone title	xx/yy/zz	Explain why milestone date is critical to project
...	...	...

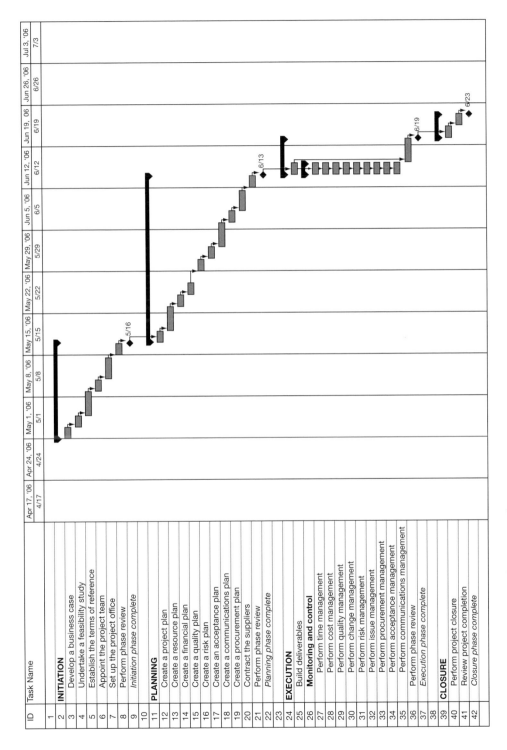

Figure 2.3 Summarized project plan

Then list any external dependencies and their criticality to the project. External dependencies are activities within the project which are likely to impact on or be impacted by an activity external to the project. (See Table 2.17.)

Table 2.17 Project dependencies

Project activity	Impacts on	Is impacted by	Criticality	Date
Planned activity	External activity	External activity	Low / medium / high	xx / yy / zz
...	...	...	...	...

A detailed project plan will be completed during the project planning phase.

Resource plan

Describe the level of resource required for the project by listing the roles, their start dates, end dates and the percentage of time that they will be allocated to the project as in Table 2.18.

Table 2.18 Project resources

Role	Start date	End date	% effort
Project role	xx / yy / zzz	xx / yy / zzz	xx / yy / zzz
...	...	...	...

A detailed resource plan will be completed during the project planning phase.

Financial plan

Summarize the project as specified in the business case, using Table 2.19.

Table 2.19 Project finances

Category	Cost	Value
People	Salaries of project staff Contractors and outsourced parties Training courses	$ x $ x $ x
Physical	Building premises for project team Equipment and materials Tools (computers, cabling, phones etc)	$ x $ x $ x
Marketing	Advertising/branding Promotional materials PR and communications	$ x $ x $ x
Organizational	Operational downtime Short-term loss in productivity Cultural change	$ x $ x Describe
...	...	...

A detailed financial plan will be completed during the project planning phase.

Quality plan

Summarize the management processes required to ensure the success of the project, using Table 2.20.

Table 2.20 Project processes

Process	Description
Time management	Summary of how the process will be undertaken
Cost management	...
Quality management	
Change management	
Risk management	
Issue management	
Procurement management	
Acceptance management	
Communications management	
...	

A detailed quality plan will be completed during the project planning phase.

List all project considerations

Project risks

Summarize the most apparent risks associated with the project by completing Table 2.21.

Table 2.21 Project risks

Risk description	Risk likelihood	Risk impact	Action to be taken to mitigate risk
Inability to recruit skilled resource	Low	Very high	Outsource project to a company with proven industry experience and appropriately skilled staff
Technology solution is unable to deliver required results	Medium	High	Complete a pilot project to prove the full technology solution
Additional capital expenditure may be required in addition to that approved	Medium	Medium	Maintain strict capital expenditure processes during the project
...	...	...	...

A detailed risk plan will be completed during the project planning phase.

Project issues

Summarize the highest priority issues associated with the project by completing Table 2.22.

Table 2.22   Project issues

Issue description	Issue priority	Action to be taken to resolve issue
Required capital expenditure funds have not been budgeted	High	Request funding approval as part of this proposal
Required computer software is only at beta phase and has not yet been released live	Medium	Design solution based on current software version and adapt changes to solution once the final version of the software has been released
Council approval must be sought to implement the final solution	Low	Initiate the council approval process early so that it does not delay the final roll-out
...	...	...

Project assumptions

List the major assumptions made while defining the project. Examples include:

- There will be no legislative, business strategy or policy changes during this project.
- Prices of raw materials will not increase during the course of the project.
- Additional human resources will be available from the business to support the project.

Project constraints

List the major constraints identified while defining the project. Examples include:

- The financial budget allocated is fixed and does not allow for over-spend.
- There are limited technical resources available for the project.
- The solution must be implemented after-hours to minimize the operational impact on the business.

You are now ready to collate all of the materials listed in this section and create your terms of reference document for approval. The next step in the project life cycle is to appoint the project team.

2.5 APPOINT THE PROJECT TEAM

Having completed the terms of reference, you will now have a very clear understanding of the types of project roles required and number of people required to fulfil each role. The next step is to appoint people to these roles, to carry out the project. The first person appointed to the project is typically the project manager. The reason is that the project manager is responsible for ensuring that the right candidates with the right skills are appointed into the right roles within the project. The project manager will usually appoint their team leaders first and the team leaders will in turn appoint the team members, depending on the size of the project. The project manager is also responsible for appointing other key project roles, such as the quality manager, procurement manager, communications manager and project office manager.

It is no surprise that hiring the right project manager for your needs is a critical activity in the project life cycle. You need a project manager who is suitably skilled, has depth of expertise in managing similar projects and is the right cultural fit for your organization. To ensure that you appoint the right person to lead your project, you need to complete a comprehensive job description for this role. To help with this, a detailed job description for a project manager is provided in this section. This job description will help you to define the project manager's role, responsibilities, skills, experience and qualifications necessary to deliver a successful project. You may use this job description format to create job descriptions for other roles within your project.

Job description

Role

Describe the purpose of the project manager's role, for example:

> The purpose of the project manager's role is to undertake the phases, activities and tasks within specified time, cost and quality constraints to deliver the required project outcome and achieve total customer satisfaction.

Responsibilities

List the key responsibilities of the role. For instance the project manager may be responsible for:

Project initiation

- Documenting the benefits, costs and available options in a business case.
- Undertaking a feasibility study to ensure that all options are achievable.
- Creating terms of reference which specify the project objectives and scope.
- Recruiting suitably skilled and qualified project team members.
- Establishing standards and guidelines for the project.

Project planning

- Creating a project schedule, outlining the sequence of all activities and tasks.
- Defining all quality targets, standards, assurance and control procedures.
- Scheduling labour, equipment and material resources within the project.
- Budgeting financial expenditure throughout the project.
- Producing a risk plan to identify and mitigate project risks.
- Documenting the acceptance criteria for each project deliverable.
- Establishing a clear communications plan for the project.
- Outlining a strategy for the procurement of goods and services.

Project execution

- Managing the project plan and keeping stakeholders properly informed.
- Controlling expenditure to ensure delivery within the approved project budget.
- Checking that adequate quality assurance and control processes are undertaken to meet the targets specified in the quality plan.
- Overseeing the approval process for all project change requests.
- Raising project risks and recommended mitigation plans for approval.
- Resolving issues currently affecting the project.
- Procuring goods and services in accordance with the procurement plan.
- Managing the construction of all project deliverables.
- Gaining customer acceptance for each deliverable produced by the project.
- Undertaking all activities specified in the communications plan.

Project closure

- Documenting a project closure report.
- Gaining approval from the project sponsor for the closure of the project.
- Undertaking all actions necessary to close the project.
- Communicating closure of the project to all stakeholders once complete.

Organization

Depict the reporting structure of the project as an organization chart. Refer to Figure 2.2 for an example.

Relationships

Describe the key relationships between the project manager and each of the key project stakeholders. For instance:

Project sponsor

The project manager reports directly to the project sponsor on a day-to-day basis. As such, the project manager will work closely with the project sponsor to obtain advice and guidance regarding the operational delivery of the project.

Project review group

The project manager will provide the project review group with regular project status information to enable the group to make informed strategic decisions for the project. The project manager will communicate all key risks, issues and change requests to the project review group for approval.

Project leaders

The project leaders report directly to the project manager. The project manager will support each project leader by providing advice, guidance and mentoring to help them achieve their project objectives.

Project team members

The project manager will lead, motivate and inspire the project team to achieve the objectives of the project. This is done by setting clear objectives for each team leader/member and recognizing achievement when each objective has been accomplished.

Skills

Identify the skills and key competencies necessary to undertake the role. For example:

Project planning

- A detailed understanding of project planning and control techniques.
- The ability to produce a detailed project plan, including a work breakdown structure (WBS), dependencies, resources and costs.

Resource management

- Knowledge of resource planning techniques.
- Sound people management skills, with an emphasis on performance management.

Financial management

- A detailed understanding of the financial planning process.
- The ability to produce accurate and up-to-date financial forecasts throughout the project.

Quality management

- The ability to define appropriate quality targets and standards.
- Knowledge of quality assurance and control techniques to ensure that quality targets and standards are met.

Change management

- An awareness of the importance of change management in projects.
- Knowledge of effective change management processes and procedures.

Experience

Identify the level of experience required to undertake this role successfully. Experience may be defined in terms of:

- the types of projects the candidate has managed;
- the industries in which the projects were undertaken;
- the size and level of complexity of the projects undertaken;
- the number of years spent managing projects;
- the countries in which the projects were undertaken.

Qualifications

Outline the necessary qualifications required to undertake this role competently. Qualification levels include:

- high school or college qualifications;
- university or other higher educational qualifications;
- specialist qualifications.

Furthermore, identify the particular discipline that each qualification should relate to such as engineering, information technology, business management, marketing and accounting.

Personality

Describe any interpersonal characteristics required for the role. Examples of valuable interpersonal traits for a project manager include:

- friendly, open and consultative in nature;
- structured, methodical and process driven;
- inspirational, motivational and lively;
- strong determination to succeed;

- driven by own personal values;
- diplomatic but firm;
- interested in people;
- sociable and outgoing.

Performance criteria

List the key performance indicators (KPIs) which provide the basis for assessing the performance of the person in this role. Examples include:

- delivery of project outcome within time, cost, quality and scope constraints;
- percentage of achievement of all project objectives;
- percentage of realization of project benefits;
- level of customer satisfaction achieved;
- level of staff satisfaction achieved;
- number of outstanding issues upon project closure.

Work environment

Describe the work environment to inform potential candidates of the general working conditions associated with this role. Examples include:

- physical exertion (amount of time standing, sitting, bending or carrying loads);
- physical environment (working in open-plan or closed-plan offices, confined spaces);
- external environment (excessive noise, moving machinery, dust, fumes, gases);
- general environment (level of challenge, organizational change, political pressures).

Salary

Specify the expected salary range and the composition of the salary package, including commissions and benefits. For example:

The remuneration rate for this role is based on an overall package of $xxx. This comprises:

- an annual salary base of $xxx, paid monthly;
- a bonus of $xxx, paid on successful completion of each project milestone;
- allowances of $xxx for a motor vehicle, petrol and mobile phone, paid monthly.

Special conditions

List any special conditions associated with this role. For instance:

- Identify any special licences, certificates or credentials required.
- Specify whether travel is required, within or outside of the country.
- State any after-hours work requirements.

You are now ready to collate all of the materials listed in this section and create a job description for each project role. The next step in the project life cycle is to set up the project office.

2.6 SET UP THE PROJECT OFFICE

The project office is the physical premises within which administrative project staff such as the project manager and project support staff reside. The project office also contains the communications infrastructure and information technologies required to support the project.

Although it is usual for a project team to be based in one physical location, a project team may be dispersed throughout different countries around the world. In this instance, a 'virtual' project office is formed. With the modern age of technology, virtual project offices are becoming more frequent as communications issues are more easily solved through e-mail, Internet access, remote network software, mobile phones, laptop technologies and hand-held devices.

To help create your project office environment, a detailed project office checklist has been provided. This checklist itemizes the steps needed to successfully establish a project office environment. It may also be used to review your project office on a regular basis to ensure that it continues to support the project as originally planned.

Project office checklist

Project details

Project name:	*Name of the project*
Project manager:	*Name of the project manager responsible for the project*
Project office manager:	*Name of the project office manager responsible for the project office*

Establish premises

- Were the requirements for the physical premises documented?
- Have the physical premises for the project been established?
- Are the premises located in a practical location?
- Do the premises meet the requirements as originally documented?
- Is there a formal contract for the lease / purchase / use of the premises?
- Do the premises provide sufficient capacity for the project?
- Will the premises continue to be available if the project is delayed?
- Do the premises require additional fit-out (eg partitions, cabling, air conditioning)?
- Are the on-site facilities sufficient (eg number of meeting rooms, bathrooms)?

Procure equipment

Office equipment

- Do the project team have the required office equipment available to manage the project (eg computer hardware, Project Planning and financial software, projectors, fax machines, printers, scanners, copiers)?
- Are maintenance contracts in place to ensure that all equipment remains operational throughout the life of the project?
- Is spare equipment available in case of a shortage?
- Is the office equipment functioning as required?

Communications equipment

- Are there sufficient voice and data communications technologies (such as computer networks, e-mail, Internet access, remote network software, mobile phones, laptops and hand-held devices)?
- Is video conferencing equipment required?
- Is all equipment functioning as required?

Define roles

- Have the following roles been appointed?
  - project sponsor / customer;
  - project manager;
  - project office manager;
  - procurement manager;
  - communications manager;
  - quality manager;
  - team leader(s).
- Have formal job descriptions been defined and agreed for all key project roles?
- Does each job description adequately describe the role, responsibilities and performance criteria?
- Have suitably skilled staff been appointed to each of the roles identified?

Implement standards and processes

Standards

Have the following standards been defined?

- quality standards;
- planning standards;
- acceptance standards;
- reporting standards;
- documentation standards;
- other relevant standards (eg ISO).

Processes

Have the following processes been defined?

- time management process;
- cost management process;
- quality management process;
- change management process;
- risk management process;
- issue management process;
- procurement management process;
- acceptance management process;
- communications management process.

Create templates

Have the following templates been created?

Initiation
- Business case.
- Feasibility study.
- Terms of reference.
- Job description.

Planning
- Project plan.
- Resource plan.
- Financial plan.
- Quality plan.
- Risk plan.
- Acceptance plan.
- Communications plan.

- Procurement plan.
- Statement of work.
- Request for information (RFI).
- Request for proposal (RFP).
- Supplier contract.
- Tender register.

Execution

- Timesheet form, timesheet register.
- Expense form, expense register.
- Quality form, quality register.
- Change form, change register.
- Risk form, risk register.
- Issue form, issue register.
- Purchase order form, procurement register.
- Project status report, communications register.
- Acceptance form, acceptance register.

Closure

- Project closure report.
- Post-implementation review (PIR).

Offer services

Are the project office staff adequately performing the following services:

- maintaining project plans by recording actuals against baseline and periodically calculating accurate forecasts?
- completing regular project status reports, distributing them to the appropriate project stakeholders and filing all project documentation efficiently?
- maintaining the project timesheet, expense, quality, change, risk, issue, procurement, communications and acceptance registers?
- conducting regular project reviews to ensure that time, cost and quality are being monitored and controlled effectively?
- providing advice, guidance, mentoring, training and support for project team leaders?

2.7 PERFORM A PHASE REVIEW

At the end of the initiation phase, a phase review is performed. This is a checkpoint to ensure that the project has achieved its stated objectives as planned. A phase review form is completed to formally request approval to proceed to the next phase of a project. Phase review forms should be completed at the end of the following project phases:

- project initiation;
- project planning;
- project execution.

It is not necessary to complete a phase review form at the end of the project closure phase as approval to close the project is covered in the project closure report. The phase review form should describe the status of the:

- overall project;
- project schedule;
- project expenses;
- project staffing;
- project deliverables;
- project risks;
- project issues.

Phase review forms should be completed by the project manager and approved by the project sponsor. To obtain approval, the project manager will usually present the current status of the project to the project board for consideration. The project board (chaired by the project sponsor) may decide to cancel the project, undertake further work within the existing project phase or grant approval to begin the next phase of the project.

A phase review form for the project initiation phase is provided as Figure 2.4.

PROJECT DETAILS

Project name: Report prepared by:

Project manager: Report preparation date:

Project sponsor: Reporting period:

Project description:

[Summarize the overall project achievements, risks and issues experienced to date.]

OVERALL STATUS

Overall status: *[Description]*

Project schedule: *[Description]*

Project expenses: *[Description]*

Project deliverables: *[Description]*

Project risks: *[Description]*

Project issues: *[Description]*

Project changes: *[Description]*

REVIEW DETAILS

Figure 2.4   Phase review form for the initiation phase

Review category	Review question	Answer	Variance
Schedule	Was the phase completed to schedule?	[Y/N]	
Expenses	Was the phase completed within budgeted cost?	[Y/N]	
Deliverables:	Deliverables:		
Business case:	Was a business case approved?	[Y/N]	
Feasibility study:	Was a feasibility study approved?	[Y/N]	
Terms of reference:	Were terms of reference approved?	[Y/N]	
Project team appointed:	Were suitably skilled staff recruited to project roles?	[Y/N]	
Risks:	Are there any outstanding project risks?	[Y/N]	
Issues:	Are there any outstanding project issues?	[Y/N]	
Changes:	Are there any outstanding project changes?	[Y/N]	

APPROVAL DETAILS

Supporting documentation:

[Reference any supporting documentation used to substantiate the review details above.]

Project sponsor

Signature: _____   Date: __/__/__

THIS PROJECT HAS BEEN APPROVED TO PROCEED TO THE PROJECT PLANNING PHASE

Figure 2.4 *continued*

3

Project planning

3.1 INTRODUCTION

Now that the project has been properly defined and the project team appointed, you are ready to plan the project in detail. The project planning phase involves creating a suite of planning documents which help guide the project team through the remaining phases of the project. The activities outlined in Figure 3.1 need to be completed.

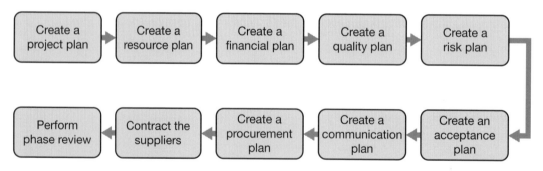

Figure 3.1   Project planning activities

When undertaking smaller projects, you may wish to combine these plans into a single planning document for approval by your sponsor. For larger projects, you will need to create each of these documents separately in the order shown, to ensure that the project activities are properly sequenced.

Regardless of the project size, the most important document created during the planning phase is the project plan. This document is referred to frequently throughout the execution phase of the project to ensure that the project is on track. A well-defined project plan will ensure that the project manager has a clear view of the activities and milestones required to meet the customer's expectations.

Project managers often fall into the trap of creating a comprehensive project plan, but failing to create the other planning documents required to monitor and control the project. As a result they suffer from inadequate resources, lack of funding, poor deliverable quality, unforeseen risks, lack of customer acceptance, poor communications, inefficient procurement and under-performing suppliers. To ensure that your project is well planned and does not experience these symptoms, you need to complete each of the activities listed in this section.

3.2 CREATE A PROJECT PLAN

The project plan is the central document by which the project is formally managed. A project plan lists the activities, tasks and resources required to complete a project and realize the business benefits outlined in the business case. A typical project plan includes:

- a description of the major phases undertaken to complete the project;
- a schedule of the activities, tasks, durations, dependencies, resources and time-frames;
- a list of the assumptions and constraints identified during the planning process.

To create a project plan, the following steps are undertaken:

- Reiterate the project scope.
- Identify the project milestones, phases, activities and tasks.
- Quantify the effort required for each task.
- Allocate project resource to each task.
- Construct a project schedule.
- List any planning dependencies, assumptions and constraints.

Although a summarized project plan will already have been specified in the business case, a detailed project plan is not created until the scope has been defined within the terms of reference and the key members of the project team have been appointed. The completion of the detailed project plan is the first step in the project planning phase, prior to the creation of a quality plan and the appointment of a preferred supplier.

The project plan is constantly referenced throughout the project. During project execution, the project manager tracks task completion, effort spent and total cost using the project plan. He or she also uses it to forecast completion dates for each activity and ensure that the project is delivered to schedule. During project closure, the project manager will ensure that all planned activities have been completed as listed in the project plan. An independent party will then review the project plan to determine whether the project delivered within the estimates agreed with the customer.

The following sections describe in plain text how to create a project plan for your project.

Define the planning basis

Scope

The first step towards creating a project plan is to reconfirm the project scope, as defined in the terms of reference. The scope defines the boundaries within which all project activities and tasks are to be completed.

Phases

Next, list and describe the major phases within the project. A phase is a set of activities to be undertaken to deliver a substantial portion of an overall project. An example is shown as Table 3.1.

Table 3.1 Project phases

Phase	Description	Sequence
Project initiation	During this phase, a business problem or opportunity is identified and a business case which provides various solution options is defined. A feasibility study is then conducted to investigate the likelihood of each solution option addressing the business problem, and a final recommended solution is put forward. Once the recommended solution is approved, a project is initiated to deliver the approved solution. Terms of reference are completed, which outline the objectives, scope and structure of the new project, and a project manager is appointed. The project manager recruits the project team and establishes a project office environment.	#1
Project planning	This phase involves the creation of a: • project plan outlining the activities, tasks, dependencies and timeframes; • resource plan listing the labour, equipment and materials required; • financial plan identifying the labour, equipment and materials costs; • quality plan providing quality targets, assurance and control measures; • risk plan highlighting potential risks and actions to be taken to mitigate those risks; • acceptance plan listing the criteria to be met to gain customer acceptance; • communications plan describing the information needed to inform stakeholders; • procurement plan identifying products to be sourced from external suppliers.	#2
Project execution	This phase involves the execution of the plans created during the project planning phase. While each plan is being executed, a series of management processes are undertaken to monitor and control the deliverables being output by the project.	#3
Project closure	This phase involves releasing the final deliverables to the customer, handing over project documentation to the business, terminating supplier contracts, releasing project resources and communicating the closure of the project to all stakeholders. The last remaining step is to undertake a post-implementation review to quantify the level of project success and identify any lessons learnt for future projects.	#4

Milestones

Now list and describe the key project milestones using Table 3.2. A milestone is a major event in a project, and often represents the completion of a set of project activities.

Table 3.2   Project milestones

Milestone	Description	Milestone date
Quality plan approved	A quality plan has been documented and approved by the project sponsor. It identifies the quality assurance and quality control techniques required to ensure and control the quality of all project deliverables and processes.	xx/yy/zz
Communications plan approved	A communications plan has been documented and approved by the project sponsor. It identifies the information to be distributed to stakeholders, the methods of distributing the information, the frequency of distribution and responsibilities of each person in the project team for distributing the information.	xx/yy/zz
Preferred supplier contracted	A formal tender process is undertaken to identify a short-list of capable suppliers and select a preferred supplier. The tender process involves creating a statement of work, a request for information and request for proposal document to obtain sufficient information from each potential supplier and select the preferred supplier. Once a preferred supplier has been chosen, a contract is agreed between the project team and the supplier for the delivery of the requisite products.	xx/yy/zz
...	...	...

Activities

List and describe the key activities in the project. An activity is a set of tasks that are required to be undertaken to complete a portion of a project. See Table 3.3.

Table 3.3 Project activities

Phase	Activity	Description	Sequence
Project planning	Develop quality plan	Produce a document describing quality assurance and quality control processes and review activities to be undertaken.	After the project plan but before the formulation of supplier contracts
…	…	…	…

Tasks

List all key tasks required to undertake each activity in the project. A task is an item of work to be completed within a project. See Table 3.4.

Table 3.4 Project tasks

Phase	Activity	Task	Sequence
Project planning	Develop quality plan	Identify quality targets Identify quality assurance techniques Identify quality control techniques Document quality plan	1st 2nd 3rd 4th
…	…	…	…

Effort

For each task listed above, quantify the likely 'effort' required to complete the task. See Table 3.5.

Table 3.5 Project effort

Task	Effort
Identify quality targets Identify quality assurance techniques Identify quality control techniques Document quality plan	no. days no. days no. days no. days
…	…

Resources

For each task listed, identify the human resources required to complete the task. See Table 3.6.

Table 3.6   Project resources

Task	Resource
Identify quality targets	name
Identify quality assurance techniques	name
Identify quality control techniques	name
Document quality plan	name
...	...

Create a project schedule

Schedule

Create a detailed project schedule, listing each of the phases, activities and tasks required to complete the project. See the example in Figure 3.2.

Dependencies

Dependencies are logical relationships between phases, activities or tasks which influence the way that a project will be undertaken. Dependencies may be internal to the project (between project activities) or external to the project (between a project activity and a business activity). Overall, there are four types of dependency:

- finish-to-start (the item this activity depends on must finish before this activity can start);
- finish-to-finish (the item this activity depends on must finish before this activity can finish);
- start-to-start (the item this activity depends on must start before this activity can start);
- start-to-finish (the item this activity depends on must start before this activity can finish).

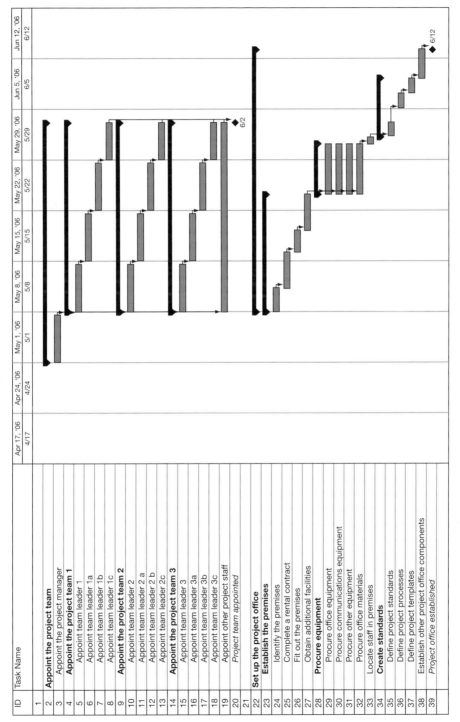

Figure 3.2 Detailed project schedule

List all project dependencies using Table 3.7.

Table 3.7 Project dependencies

Activity	Depends on	Dependency type
Set up project office	Appoint project team	Finish-to-finish
…	…	…

In this example, the activity 'Appoint project team' must finish before activity 'Set up project office' can finish.

Assumptions

Identify any planning assumptions made during this planning process. For example, it may be assumed that:

- the project will not change in scope;
- the resources identified will be available upon request;
- approved funding will be available upon request.

Constraints

Identify any planning constraints identified. For example:

- the project team must create all project deliverables using the approved funding, resources, materials and equipment only;
- the project team must create all project deliverables within normal working hours only.

You are now ready to collate all of the materials listed in this section and create your project plan document. This document forms the basis upon which the project is measured, and it will be referred to throughout the project life cycle. The next step in the project life cycle is to create a resource plan.

3.3 CREATE A RESOURCE PLAN

A resource plan describes the physical resource required to complete a project. This includes a list of the types of resource required, such as labour, equipment and materials, as well as a schedule identifying when each resource will be utilized. A resource plan is created after the project plan has been defined. Although summarized resource information may be described in the business case, feasibility study, terms of reference and project plan documents, a detailed resource plan cannot be created until every activity and task in the project plan has been identified. Following the completion of the resource plan, it will be possible to finalize the financial plan, as the fixed cost portion of the project will have been identified.

To create a resource plan, the following steps are undertaken:

● List the general types of resources to be utilized on the project.
● Identify the number and purpose of each type of resource required.
● Identify when each resource will be utilized, by completing a resource schedule.
● Assign the resources to project activities, by completing a resource usage table.

To create a resource plan for small projects, you can simply take each activity listed in the project plan and assign resources to it. This is relatively easy using a planning tool such as Microsoft Project. For larger more complex projects, a full resource plan (as described in the following section) should be completed to ensure that the amount and type of allocated resources are both accurate and timely.

List the resources

To create a comprehensive resource plan, you will first need to list the types and number of resources required to complete the project. A 'resource' is defined as the labour, equipment and materials used to complete each activity in the project.

Labour

Summarize the roles, responsibilities and skill-sets required to complete the project. This includes the roles of current staff appointed, further roles to be appointed, the roles of external business staff involved with the project and the roles of external suppliers. In short, every role in the project should be defined using Table 3.8.

Table 3.8   Labour listing

Role	No.	Summarized responsibilities	Summarized skills	Start date	End date
Project manager	1	Delivering the approved solution to meet the full requirements of the customer	Time management Cost management Quality management People management	xx/yy/zz	xx/yy/zz
…	…	…	…	…	…

In Table 3.8 the 'No.' column represents the number of full-time equivalent people required to undertake the role. For instance a project might require one project manager, one project administrator and 10 staff. The 'Start date' and 'End date' columns identify how long the role will exist for. In the instance of the project manager, the start date will be during the project initiation phase, and the end date will be soon after the completion of the project closure report in the project closure phase.

Equipment

Now that you have identified the labour required to undertake the project, it is necessary to list in detail all of the items of equipment needed. This includes computers, furniture, building facilities, machinery, vehicles and any other items of equipment needed to complete the project. Each item of equipment should be listed in Table 3.9, including a description of the purpose of each item, the specification of the item and the period that the item is needed for the project.

Table 3.9 Equipment listing

Item	No.	Purpose	Specification	Start date	End date
Laptop	1	To enable the project manager to plan, monitor and control the project both on and off site	High processing speed and wide screen	xx/yy/zz	xx/yy/zz
...	...	...	...	...	...

In Table 3.9 the 'No.' column represents the number of equipment items required. The 'Start date' and 'End date' columns identify how long the equipment is required for.

Materials

Now identify all of the generic materials required to undertake the project, including stationery, computer consumables, building materials, power, water and gas. Each item of material should be defined by listing its components and the period of required usage. Complete Table 3.10.

Table 3.10 Materials listing

Item	Components	Amount	Start date	End date
Computer consumables	Printer cartridges Printer paper CDs for file backup	No.	xx/yy/zz	xx/yy/zz
…	…	…	…	…

In Table 3.10, the 'Amount' column describes the approximate quantity of each item of material. The 'Start date' and 'End date' columns identify how long the materials are required for.

Build a resource schedule

Schedule

Now that all of the resources have been listed, you need to identify when each resource will be used by the project. You can do this by creating a detailed resource schedule. The resource schedule enables a project manager to identify the quantity required of each type of resource on a daily, weekly or monthly basis. For simplicity, a sample monthly resource schedule is shown as Table 3.11.

Table 3.11 Resource schedule

Month													
Resource	Jan	Feb	Mar	Apr	May	Jun	Jul	Aug	Sept	Oct	Nov	Dec	Total
Labour • Project manager • *Labour type*	*Quantity*												
Equipment • Computer • *Equipment type*													
Materials • Printer cartridges • *Material type*													
Total													

Assumptions

List any assumptions made during this resource planning exercise. For instance:

> It is assumed that the resource requirements and the delivery dates will not change throughout the project. It is also assumed that resources listed will be available as required to undertake the associated project activities.

Risks

List any risks identified during this resource planning exercise. For example:

- key staff resign during the project;
- further training is required to complete the tasks allocated;
- budgetary constraints lead to inferior resources being allocated;
- equipment is not delivered on time, as per the resource schedule.

You are now ready to collate all of the materials listed in this section and create your resource plan document. The next step in the project life cycle is to create a financial plan.

3.4 CREATE A FINANCIAL PLAN

A financial plan identifies the financial resources required to undertake a project. This includes:

- a list of the costs/expenses likely to be incurred on the project such as labour, equipment, materials and administration costs;
- a schedule identifying when each respective cost is likely to be incurred;
- a calculation of the total cost of each activity outlined in the project plan.

A financial plan is created after the resource plan has been defined. Although summarized financial information may be described in the business case, feasibility study, terms of reference and project plan documents, a detailed financial plan cannot be created until every activity and resource within the project plan and resource plan have been identified. To create a financial plan, the following steps are undertaken:

- List the types of costs to be incurred on the project.
- Identify the unit cost for each cost type.
- Identify when the costs will be incurred by completing an expense schedule.
- Identify the cost per activity by completing an activity expense schedule.

To create a financial plan for small projects, you can simply assign a planned amount of expenditure to each activity listed in the project plan. This is relatively easy using a planning tool such as Microsoft Project. For larger, more complex projects, a full financial plan (as described in the following section) should be completed to ensure that the allocated amount of financial expenditure is both accurate and appropriate.

Forecast the costs

This section itemizes the financial expenditure required to undertake the project.

Labour

List each of the roles within the project and specify their per-unit costs, as in Table 3.12.

Table 3.12   Labour costs

Role	Unit cost
Project sponsor	Cost per hour
Project manager	Cost per hour
Project administrator	Cost per hour
…	…

Note: All roles that require project expenditure should be listed here, including external consultants, contractors and suppliers.

Equipment

List each item of equipment required by the project and their per-unit costs, as in Table 3.13.

Table 3.13 Equipment costs

Equipment item	Unit cost
Computers	Cost per item
Furniture	Cost per item
Building facilities	Cost per item
Machinery	Cost per item
Vehicles	Cost per item
…	…

Materials

List each type of material required by the project and their per-unit costs, as in Table 3.14.

Table 3.14 Material costs

Material item	Unit cost
Stationery	Cost per item
Computer consumables	Cost per item
Building materials	Cost per item
Power	Cost per item
Water	Cost per item
…	…

Administration

List any administrative costs to be incurred by the project and their associated costs, as in Table 3.15.

Table 3.15 Administrative costs

Administration item	Unit cost
Legal fees	Cost per hour
Insurance fees	Cost per hour
Lending fees	Cost per hour
Accounting fees	Cost per hour
...	...

Other

List any other costs to be incurred and their associated costs in Table 3.16.

Table 3.16 Other costs

Item	Unit cost
Other item	Cost per hour
...	...

Contingency

Finally, identify any contingent costs to be taken into account. 'Contingent costs' are those that are unpredictable during the project planning phase but have been reasonably included to mitigate the risk of the project exceeding budget.

Build an expense schedule

Schedule

Now that the expense items have been listed, you need to decide when each expense is likely to occur. Table 3.17 enables you to identify the month in which the expense occurs, as well as the total cost of each expense type. You may wish to produce a weekly view to manage expenses at a more detailed level.

Table 3.17 Expense schedule

Month													
Expense type	**Jan**	**Feb**	**Mar**	**Apr**	**May**	**Jun**	**Jul**	**Aug**	**Sept**	**Oct**	**Nov**	**Dec**	**Total**
Labour • Project manager • *Expense type*	*Total expense ($/£/ other)*												
Equipment • Computers • *Expense type*													
Materials • Stationery • *Expense type*													
Administration • Legal fees • *Expense type*													
Contingency • *Expense type*													
Total													

Usage

In addition to understanding the total cost per expense type, it is also important to understand the cost of undertaking each activity (such as the total cost of building the deliverables). Table 3.18 allows you to quantify the total monthly cost of each activity listed in the project plan. You may wish to produce a weekly view to manage expenses at a more detailed level.

Table 3.18 Activity expense schedule

Month												
Activity	**Jan**	**Feb**	**Mar**	**Apr**	**May**	**Jun**	**Jul**	**Aug**	**Sept**	**Oct**	**Nov**	**Dec**	**Total**
Initiation ● Appoint team ● *Activity*	*Total expense ($/£/ other)*												
Planning ● Develop plans ● *Activity*													
Execution ● Build deliverables ● *Activity*													
Closure ● Customer sign-off ● *Activity*													
Total													

Assumptions

Identify any planning assumptions made during this financial planning process. For example, it may be assumed that:

● the project delivery dates will not change during this project;
● the per-units will not change during this project;
● the funds listed by this financial plan will be available as required.

Risks

List any risks identified during this financial planning exercise. Examples include:

● that additional funds are required by the project, outside of the contingency allocated;
● that the project delivery dates are brought forward resulting in funding implications;
● that the equipment required is unavailable and additional costs will be incurred to secure additional equipment at short notice.

You are now ready to collate all of the materials listed in this section and create your financial plan document. The next step in the project life cycle is to create a quality plan.

3.5 CREATE A QUALITY PLAN

'Quality' can be defined as the extent to which the final deliverable conforms to the customer's requirements. Quality is usually considered from two different perspectives: the quality of each deliverable produced for the customer, and the quality of the management processes undertaken to produce each deliverable. For this reason, a quality plan not only defines the approach taken to ensure the level of quality of each deliverable, it also highlights the management processes required to influence deliverable quality, such as change, risk and issue management.

To create a quality plan, the following steps are undertaken:

- Define the term 'quality' in regards to this project.
- Identify the quality targets to be met.
- Describe the quality assurance and control techniques to be undertaken.
- Define the processes required to achieve the quality targets specified.

A quality plan is created during the project planning phase after the project plan, resource plan and financial plan have been identified. As the quality plan summarizes the quality targets to be met and the management processes to be undertaken, it is referred to throughout the entire project.

Define deliverable quality

The first step towards developing a comprehensive quality plan is to identify how you will assure and control the quality of deliverables within the project. To do this, you will need to define the term 'quality', set quality targets and list quality assurance and quality control activities.

Definition

To ensure that there is a consistent understanding of the term 'quality' within the project, you should formally define the term as follows:

Quality is the extent to which the final deliverable conforms to the customer requirements.

Quality targets

For each project requirement and deliverable, identify the quality targets that, once met, will ensure that the deliverable meets the requirements of the customer. See Table 3.19 for an example.

Table 3.19 Quality targets

Quality targets			
Project requirement	**Project deliverable**	**Quality criteria**	**Quality standards**
New financial management solution with accounts receivable and payables processes	Implementation of Oracle Financials General Ledger (GL), Accounts Payable (AP) and Accounts Receivable (AR) system modules	System functionality: • GL tested & installed. • AP tested & installed. • AR tested & installed. System performance • System up-time. • System response time. • Data migrated from old system.	System functionality: • GL operational with no errors. • AP operational with no errors. • AR operational with no errors. System performance • 99.9% system uptime. • <5 second response times. • 100% data accuracy.
...	...	...	...

Quality assurance plan

To provide the customer with assurance that the quality targets specified above will be met, quality assurance (QA) techniques should be defined. QA techniques are the preventative steps taken to eliminate any variances in the quality of the deliverable produced from the quality targets set. QA is often undertaken at a summarized level of the project by an external project resource. Examples of techniques used to assure the quality of deliverables include:

- **Reviewing historical data:** understanding other related projects (either currently under way or recently completed) and the quality issues encountered with those projects will enable the quality manager to identify potential quality issues within this project.
- **Defining requirements:** by documenting a comprehensive set of customer requirements, you will gain a greater understanding of the level of deliverable quality required to achieve total customer satisfaction.
- **Defining standards:** by defining a specific set of quality criteria and standards, the project team will clearly understand the level of quality to be achieved.
- **Recruiting skilled staff:** using skilled staff will directly affect the quality of the deliverables produced. Appropriately skilled staff should have the knowledge, skills and experience required to undertake the tasks allocated in the project plan with minimal training, to achieve the level of quality desired.

- **Undertaking quality reviews:** independent reviews to assess the overall quality of each deliverable can provide the customer with confidence that the project is on track and likely to produce a deliverable that meets the requirements.
- **Implementing change control:** changes to scope often have an effect on the level of quality delivered. Through the identification of a clear change control process, only changes which are absolutely necessary will be adopted by the project for implementation.

Identify from Table 3.20 the techniques required to assure the customer that the quality targets will be met.

Table 3.20   Quality assurance plan

QA plan		
Technique	**Description**	**Frequency**
Recruit skilled staff	We will recruit skilled staff to assure deliverable quality by: • ensuring that staff allocated to the project have at least three years' commercial experience in similar projects within this business field; • appointing two senior managers from the existing business who understand the business requirements in detail; • appointing two technical consultants to ensure that the technology deliverables of this project meet the quality targets.	Throughout project
Undertake quality reviews	We will review the quality of deliverables by: • appointing an independent resource to perform monthly quality reviews for all key project deliverables; • appointing a quality manager in the project who is responsible for the quality of the deliverables produced by the project.	Monthly
...	...	...

Quality control plan

In addition to undertaking QA to improve deliverable quality, a series of quality control (QC) techniques may be implemented. QC is defined as the curative steps taken to eliminate any variances in the quality of the deliverable produced from the quality targets set. QC techniques are often undertaken at a detailed level of the project by an internal project resource. The types of techniques used to 'control' deliverable quality are:

- **Peer reviews:** the process of requiring project team members to review each other's work is known to increase the level of quality of deliverables. It will also enable quality issues to be identified earlier in the project execution phase and therefore increase the likelihood of quality issues being resolved earlier.
- **Deliverable reviews:** internal project staff may undertake formal planned reviews of deliverables to ensure that they will meet the requirements of the customer.
- **Documentation reviews:** similar to deliverable reviews, this process involves the review of all project documentation at regular planned intervals in the project.
- **Phase reviews:** these are formal reviews at the end of each major project milestone to assess the activities and deliverables completed to date and gain approval from the project sponsor to continue to the next project phase.

Identify the QC techniques to be implemented to control the quality of each deliverable on the project. Table 3.21 provides an example.

Table 3.21 Quality control plan

QC plan		
Technique	**Description**	**Frequency**
Peer reviews	Implement the following peer review policy: • A team leader will be made responsible for each project deliverable. • Each team leader will be assigned a team lead 'peer' for peer reviews. • Team leaders will formally review their peer's deliverables weekly. • Team leaders will document the results of each peer review using a quality review form. • The quality manager will review the peer review process regularly to ensure that peer reviews are being undertaken regularly.	Weekly, throughout project
Phase reviews	Implement phase reviews: • At the end of each project phase, a formal phase review will be undertaken. This review will entail gaining acceptance from the project sponsor that the project has achieved its objectives to date and can progress to the next phase of the project. • To initiate a phase review, the project manager will complete a phase review form and submit it to the project review board for assessment and approval.	At the end of each project milestone
...	...	...

Define process quality

In addition to describing how you will ensure the quality of each deliverable produced for the customer, you should also describe how you are going to ensure the quality of the management processes undertaken to produce each deliverable. For each of the processes below, describe the steps involved in undertaking the process and the responsibilities of resource responsible for managing the process:

- time management process;
- cost management process;
- quality management process;
- change management process;
- risk management process;
- issue management process;
- procurement management process;
- acceptance management process;
- communications management process.

You are now ready to collate all of the materials listed in this section and create your quality plan document. The next step in the project life cycle is to create a risk plan.

3.6 CREATE A RISK PLAN

Now that the project activities, resources and financial expenditure have been planned in detail, it is time to identify and assess the level of project risk. A risk plan lists all of the foreseeable project risks and provides a set of actions required to prevent each risk from occurring and reduce its impact should it eventuate. A comprehensive risk plan includes a:

- list of the foreseeable project risks;
- rating of the likelihood of each risk occurring;
- description of the impact on the project should a risk actually occur;
- rating of the overall importance of each risk;
- set of preventative actions to be taken to reduce the likelihood of the risk occurring;
- set of contingent actions to be taken to reduce the impact should the risk eventuate;
- process for managing risk throughout the project.

A risk plan should be documented in the project planning phase to ensure that risks are mitigated prior to project execution. Immediately after the risk plan has been documented, a risk management process is initiated to monitor and control risks identified within the project. The risk management process is terminated only when the project execution phase is complete.

Identify the risks

The first step towards creating a risk plan is to identify any risks that could adversely affect the ability of the project to achieve its defined objectives. A series of risk categories is listed, and for each category, a set of potential risks are identified. A risk planning workshop may be undertaken to help key project stakeholders identify project risks. This could involve the project sponsor, project manager, project team, suppliers and in some cases even the customer. Each of the risks identified is defined and documented in detail in the risk plan.

Definition

To ensure that there is a consistent understanding of the term 'risk' within the project, it will be necessary to formally define the term as follows:

> A risk is an event that is likely to adversely affect the ability of the project to achieve the defined objectives.

Categories

Identify the likely categories of risk for this project. A risk category is a particular aspect of the project that is likely to experience a risk during the course of the project. Typical categories are:

- requirements;
- benefits;
- schedule;
- budget;
- deliverable;
- scope;
- issues;
- supplier;
- acceptance;
- communication;
- resource.

Risks

Identify the potential risks for each risk category, by completing Table 3.22. Each risk listed should be allocated a unique identification (ID) number for later reference.

Table 3.22 Risk list

Risk category	Risk description	Risk ID
Requirements	The requirements have not been clearly specified. The requirements specified do not match the customer's needs. The requirements specified are not measurable.	1.1 1.2 1.3
Benefits	The business benefits have not been identified. The business benefits are not quantifiable. The final solution delivered does not achieve the required benefits.	2.1 2.2 2.3
Schedule	The schedule does not provide enough time to complete the project. The schedule does not list all of the activities and tasks required. The schedule does not provide accurate dependencies.	3.1 3.2 3.3
Budget	The project exceeds the budget allocated. There is unaccounted expenditure on the project. There are no resources accountable for recording project spend.	4.1 4.2 4.3
Deliverables	The deliverables required by the project are not clearly defined. Clear quality criteria for each deliverable have not been defined. The deliverable produced does not meet the quality criteria defined.	5.1 5.2 5.3
Scope	The scope of the project is not clearly outlined. The project is not undertaken within the agreed scope. Project changes negatively impact on the project.	6.1 6.2 6.3
Issues	Project issues are not resolved within an appropriate timescale. Similar issues continually reappear throughout the project. Unresolved issues become new risks to the project.	7.1 7.2 7.3
Suppliers	The expectations for supplier delivery are not defined. Suppliers do not meet the expectations defined. Procurement delays impact on the project delivery timescales.	8.1 8.2 8.3
Acceptance	The criteria for accepting project deliverables are not clearly defined. Customers do not accept the final deliverables of the project. The acceptance process leaves the customer dissatisfied.	9.1 9.2 9.3
Communication	Lack of controlled communication causes project issues. Key project stakeholders are left in the dark about progress.	10.1 10.2
Resource	Staff allocated to the project are not suitably skilled. There is insufficient equipment to undertake the project. There is a shortage of materials available when required.	11.1 11.2 11.3
...	...	...

Quantify the risks

The next step is to rate the likelihood and impact of each risk happening.

Likelihood

Create a scoring system used to measure the likelihood of each risk eventuating, as in Table 3.23.

Table 3.23   Risk likelihood

Title	Score	Description
Very low	20	Highly unlikely to occur based on current information, as the circumstances likely to trigger the risk are also unlikely to occur.
Low	40	Unlikely to occur. However needs to be monitored as certain circumstances could result in this risk becoming more likely to occur during the project.
Medium	60	Likely to occur as it is clear that the risk may eventuate.
High	80	Very likely to occur, based on the circumstances of the project.
Very high	100	Highly likely to occur as the circumstances that will cause this risk to eventuate are also very likely to eventuate.

Impact

Create a scoring system used to measure the 'impact' of each risk should it occur, as in Table 3.24.

Table 3.24   Risk impact

Title	Score	Description
Very low	20	Insignificant impact on the project. It is not possible to measure the impact on the project as it is so minimal.
Low	40	Minor impact on the project. Results in less than 5 per cent deviation in scope, scheduled end-date or project budget.
Medium	60	Measurable impact on the project. Results in a 5–10 per cent deviation in scope, scheduled end-date or project budget.
High	80	Significant impact on the project. Results in a 10–25 per cent deviation in scope, scheduled end-date or project budget.
Very high	100	Major impact on the project. Results in a greater than 25 per cent deviation in scope, scheduled end-date or project budget.

Priority

The priority score may be calculated as the average of the likelihood and impact scores (ie Priority = [Likelihood + Impact] / 2). Complete Table 3.25.

Table 3.25   Risk priority

Risk ID	Likelihood	Impact	Priority	Rating
1.1	20	80	50	Medium
1.2	80	60	70	High
1.3	100	40	70	High
2.1	40	20	30	Low
2.2	90	100	95	Very high
2.3	20	80	50	Medium
...	...	...	...	...

The rating is based on the calculated priority score. Use the system in Table 3.26 to determine the rating and assign an appropriate colour code:

Table 3.26   Risk priority ratings

Priority score	Priority rating	Priority colour
0–20	Very low	White
21–40	Low	Green
41–60	Medium	Yellow
61–80	High	Orange
81–100	Very high	Red
...	...	...

Create a risk schedule

Schedule

For each risk identified, list the preventive actions required to reduce the likelihood of the risk occurring, as well as the contingent actions needed to reduce the impact to the project should the risk occur. Against each action, assign a resource responsible for undertaking the action and a date within which the action must be complete. Use Table 3.27 to collate this information. This table should be completed for every risk identified. Higher priority risks should be assigned more comprehensive actions where possible.

Table 3.27 Risk schedule

Rating	Risk ID	Preventive actions	Action resource	Action date	Contingent actions	Action resource	Action date
Very high	2.2	Clearly identify the expected business benefits	Project sponsor	*xx/yy/zz*	Measure the actual business benefits achieved by the project	Project manager	*xx/yy/zz*
High	1.2	Clearly specify the customer requirements in the quality plan	Project manager	*xx/yy/zz*	Assess the requirements after the deliverable has been produced, measure any deviation and enhance the deliverable to meet the requirements	Project manager	*xx/yy/zz*
High	1.3	Clearly specify the quality criteria used to determine that the stated requirements for each deliverable have been met	Quality manager	*xx/yy/zz*	Assess the quality criteria after the deliverable has been produced, measure any deviation and enhance the deliverable to meet the quality criteria set	Quality manager	*xx/yy/zz*
...	...	...	...	...	...	...	...

You are now ready to collate all of the materials listed in this section and create your risk plan document. The next step in the project life cycle is to create an acceptance plan.

3.7 CREATE AN ACCEPTANCE PLAN

'Acceptance' is defined as gaining agreement from the customer that the deliverables produced by the project meet the criteria defined by the customer. These criteria relate to the quality and cost of deliverables as well as the timeframes within which they are produced. An acceptance plan includes:

- a list of the milestones to be achieved and deliverables to be produced;
- a set of criteria and standards for the acceptance of deliverables by the customer;
- a plan outlining how the deliverables will be reviewed to determine whether or not they meet the criteria and adhere to the standards set by the customer;
- a process for gaining customer acceptance once the deliverables have been produced.

The acceptance plan is an important document in a project. It is usually constructed towards the end of the project planning phase after the project plan, resource plan, financial plan, quality plan and risk plan have been documented. The acceptance plan is referred to throughout the execution phase as it is used to confirm that each deliverable produced is complete and ready for customer acceptance. It is also referred to during the closure phase as part of the project closure report and post-implementation review.

Identify the acceptance criteria

Definition

To ensure that there is a consistent understanding of the term 'acceptance' within the project, you should formally define the term. We define acceptance as follows:

> Acceptance is defined as gaining agreement from the customer that the deliverables produced by the project meet the criteria defined by the customer.

Milestones

List the project milestones and deliverables for which customer acceptance will be sought:

Table 3.28 Acceptance milestones

Milestone		Deliverable	
Name	**Description**	**Name**	**Description**
Financial system upgraded	Implement the software package on new hardware	Software package installed	Implementation of General Ledger (GL), Accounts Payable (AP) and Accounts Receivable (AR) software
...	...	...	...

Criteria

Identify the criteria and standards to be met to achieve final customer acceptance for each deliverable.

Table 3.29 Acceptance criteria

Deliverable	Criteria	Standards
Software package installed	*System functionality*: • GL tested and installed. • AP tested and installed. • AR tested and installed. *System Performance* • System up-time. • System response time. • Data transferred.	*System functionality*: • GL operational with no errors. • AP operational with no errors. • AR operational with no errors. *System Performance* • 99.9% system uptime. • <1 second response times. • 100% data accuracy.
...	...	...

The criteria and standards listed must convince the customer that the deliverables produced can be measured sufficiently to ensure that the requirements are fully met. Although the criteria listed primarily address 'deliverable' quality, other types of criteria may be used such as:

• the quality of new processes delivered by the project;
• the timeliness of the deliverables and processes;
• the ability of the project to produce the deliverables within budget.

Build an acceptance schedule

Schedule

Create a schedule of reviews needed to ensure that the deliverables produced by the project meet the criteria and standards already defined. An example is shown in Table 3.30.

Table 3.30   Acceptance schedule

Completion milestone	Deliverable	Date	Acceptance Review method	Reviewers	Date
Financial system upgraded	Software package installed	xx/yy/zz	Physical inspection Software testing Data accuracy review	Systems tester Project manager Data quality manager Customer advocate Independent advisor	xx/yy/zz
...	...	...	...	...	...

Note:

● The completion date is the planned date on which the deliverable will be 100 per cent complete and ready for customer acceptance.
● The review method is the technique used to assess whether or not the quality criteria have been met.
● The reviewers are the people jointly responsible for undertaking the review.
● The acceptance date is the planned date for acceptance of the deliverable by the customer, following the completion of the acceptance review.

Assumptions

List any planning assumptions made during this acceptance planning exercise. For example it may be assumed that:

● there will be no changes to project requirements during this project;
● the acceptance criteria will not change during this project;
● the reviewers will be available to conduct the reviews as required.

Risks

List any risks identified during this acceptance planning exercise. For example:

- the acceptance criteria may not be directly aligned with the customer's requirements;
- the acceptance reviews undertaken may not provide adequate confidence that the deliverables meet the acceptance criteria listed above;
- the resource allocated to undertake the acceptance review may not be appropriately skilled to complete each review as required.

You are now ready to collate all of the materials listed in this section and create your acceptance plan document. The next step in the project life cycle is to create a communications plan.

3.8 CREATE A COMMUNICATIONS PLAN

A communications plan describes the information to be disseminated to all project stakeholders to keep them regularly informed of the progress of the project. A clear communications plan is vital to the success of the project, as it helps ensure that all project resources and stakeholders are working towards the same project objectives, and that any hurdles are overcome in a planned and informed manner.

The communications plan contains the following information:

- the information requirements of each project stakeholder;
- a schedule of the communication events, methods and release dates;
- a matrix highlighting the resource involved in each communication event;
- a clear process for undertaking each communication event within the project.

After the communications plan has been agreed, the communications management process is invoked to ensure that all communication events are undertaken in a clear and coordinated manner.

Identify the communications requirements

Stakeholders

The first step towards creating an effective communications plan is to list the project 'stakeholders'. A communications stakeholder is a person or entity within or outside the project requiring regular information about the project. For instance, a project sponsor will be interested in the overall progress of the project, whereas an external body may be concerned with legislative or regulatory compliance. List all communications stakeholder groups who require information during the project. Examples include:

- project sponsor;
- project review group;
- project manager;
- project leader;
- project member;
- quality manager;
- procurement manager;
- communications manager;
- project office manager;
- other project resources;
- other external bodies.

Requirements

For all stakeholders identified, describe the information required to keep them appropriately informed of the progress of the project. Table 3.31 provides examples.

Table 3.31 Communications requirements

Stakeholder	Information requirement
Project sponsor	Project status information (schedule, budget and scope) Understanding of critical project risks and issues Information required to approve each project phase.
Project review group	Project status information (schedule, budget and scope) Detailed knowledge of important risks and issues Information regarding proposed project changes (for approval).
Project manager	Detailed project status information (schedule, budget and scope) Understanding of current project deliverable quality Detailed knowledge of all risks, issues and change requests.
Project leader	Project activity and task status information Day-to-day knowledge of issues and risks identified.
Project members	Status of the activities and tasks they are dependent on Awareness of events which may affect their ability to undertake their role.
Quality manager	Progress of each deliverable against quality standards and criteria set Detailed understanding of all quality issues for resolution.
…	…

Build a communications schedule

Schedule

It is now time to describe each communication event, including its purpose, method and frequency by completing Table 3.32.

Table 3.32 Communications schedule

ID	Event	Description	Purpose	Method	Frequency	Date(s)
1.1	Project team meetings	Meeting involving all team members to discuss the work in progress / recently completed / coming up	To keep the team informed of the project status and ensure that issues, risks or changes are raised accordingly	Verbal	Weekly	*xx/yy/zz*
1.2	Quality review meetings	Regular meetings involving the quality manager and quality review staff to ascertain the level of quality of all project deliverables	To ensure that quality issues are identified early, thereby providing time to enhance the quality of each deliverable and meet the quality criteria	Verbal	Monthly	*xx/yy/zz*
1.3	Stage-gate review meetings	Formal meetings held at the end of each phase to identify the overall status of the project, the quality of the deliverables produced and any outstanding risks, issues or changes	To control the progress of the project through each phase in the project life cycle, thereby enhancing its likelihood of success	Verbal	Weekly	*xx/yy/zz*
1.4	Change approval group meetings	Formal meetings held regularly to review change requests	To provide a formal process for the approval of project changes	Verbal	Fortnightly	*xx/yy/zz*
1.5	Customer acceptance meetings	Held with the customer to obtain final acceptance of a set of completed project deliverables	To provide a controlled process for the acceptance of deliverables and ensure that customer requirements are met	Verbal	Following deliverable's completion	*xx/yy/zz*
1.6	Supplier performance meetings	Regular meetings with each supplier to discuss performance issues and product delivery status	To provide a forum within which to assess supplier performance and resolve supplier issues	Verbal	Monthly	*xx/yy/zz*
1.7	Status reports	Reports providing the status of the schedule, budget, risks and issues	To keep all key project stakeholders informed of the status of the project	Status report	Weekly	*xx/yy/zz*
...	...	...	...	...	...	...

Matrix

Complete Table 3.33 (opposite) to help you identify the people participating in each communication event and their roles. Use the unique identifier (ID) to link events listed in Table 3.32 to the participating parties listed here.

Assumptions

List any assumptions made during the communications planning process. For example, it might be assumed that:

* the communications tools will be provided as required;
* adequate communications resources will be available when needed;
* the communications staff have the required expertise.

Risks

List any risks identified during the communications planning process. For example:

* key communications staff leave during the life of the project;
* the requirements for communication change during the project;
* communications are not undertaken effectively.

You are now ready to collate all of the materials listed in this section and create your communications plan document. The next step is to create a procurement plan.

3.9 CREATE A PROCUREMENT PLAN

A procurement plan identifies the products to be procured from external suppliers and the timeframes and methods of procurement. This includes:

* An overview of the external supply market. This will provide key stakeholders with confidence that the products do actually exist in the market and that suitable suppliers can readily provide them within the time and budget constraints.
* A full list of the products to be acquired and a detailed description of each product.
* The justification for procuring the products externally rather than internally.
* A plan outlining the timeframes for acquiring the products.
* A tender process describing how the preferred suppliers will be chosen.
* A procurement process describing how the products will be acquired from the preferred supplier. It also describes how the supplier relationship will be managed to ensure continued delivery.

It is important to note that for the purposes of this book, the term 'products' includes goods (such as computer hardware, materials and equipment) and services (such as raw labour, technical services, consultancy and management). A procurement plan should be

Table 3.33 Communications matrix

ID	Project sponsor	Project manager	Project leader	Project member	Quality manager	Procurement manager	Communications manager	Profit office manager	Other project resource	Other external body
1.1	–	A	R	R	R	R	R,M	R	R	R (Supplier)
1.2	–	R	R	–	A	–	M	R	–	R (Supplier)
1.3	A	R	–	–	–	–	M	–	–	–
1.4	A	R	–	–	R	–	M	–	–	–
1.5	R	A	R	–	–	–	M	–	–	R (Supplier)
1.6	–	R	–	–	–	A	M	–	–	–
1.7	R	A	R	–	R	R	M	R	–	–
...	...	...	...	...	...	...	...	...	...	...

Key:
A = Accountable for the communications event, develops and distributes materials and facilitates meetings.
R = Receives communications materials provided, takes part in meetings.
M = Monitors communications process and provides feedback.

created for any project that involves the acquisition of product from an external supplier. Whether it involves one or more products or suppliers, a clear plan for the acquisition of products should be documented in the form of a procurement plan. This document is formed in the latter half of the project planning phase, and relies heavily on the description of deliverables provided in the project plan and quality plan.

Identify the procurement requirements

The first step towards defining a procurement plan is to identify the products to be sourced from outside the organization. You will also need to specify the purpose of each product and the justification for procuring it externally as opposed to sourcing it internally from within the business.

Requirements

List and describe the products to be sourced from the external market place. Assign each product a product ID, define the quantities required and the budgeted cost of each. (See Table 3.34.)

Table 3.34 Procurement requirements

Product	Description	Product ID	Quantity	Budget
Computer hardware	Latest specification computer Intel PC including: • screen (19 inch monitor); • computer unit (latest Intel processor); • accessories (keyboard, mouse); • latest Windows operating system; • MS Office software suite.	CH1	*Amount*	$
Raw materials	Building construction materials, including: • wooden framing for walls • roofing materials • electrical cabling and switches.	RM1	*Amount*	$
Consultancy services	General consultancy services to assist with the management of the project, including: • quality assurance and auditing; • project office management; • accounting services.	CS1	*Amount*	$
...	...	...	...	...

Purpose

Then outline the purpose of each product as shown in Table 3.35.

Table 3.35 Product purpose

Product ID	Product	Purpose
CH1	Computer hardware	To enable project management and administrative staff to oversee the project by recording and tracking progress against project plans
RM1	Raw materials	To physically construct the deliverables to be produced by the project
CS1	Consultancy services	To provide confidence that the project will achieve the time, cost and quality targets through regular reviews and reporting.
...	...	...

Justification

Provide sound reasoning why the above products must be acquired from external suppliers as opposed to from within the existing business, using Table 3.36.

Table 3.36 Product justification

Product ID	Product	Justification
CH1	Computer hardware	There are no available PCs within the business of a suitable specification to perform the required tasks
RM1	Raw materials	The business does not currently have sufficient spare raw materials to produce the project deliverable
CS1	Consultancy services	There are no suitable human resources within the business, qualified to undertake the activities required.
...	...	...

Undertake market research

Conducting market research is critical to ensuring that the right products are readily available, at the right price and the right time. Questions such as 'Which products are available?', 'Will they meet the requirement?' and 'Are suppliers able to deliver the product at the right price within the timescales needed?' all need to be answered before the procurement plan can be completed. Undertake a thorough market research exercise, and document the results of the research programme as outlined below.

Market conditions

Assess the current market environment by answering the following types of questions:

- Is the political environment stable? Is change likely?
- What are the technology trends? Will new technologies offer new opportunities or threats?
- How many suppliers are in this particular market segment and what are their capabilities?
- Who dominates the market and why?

Available products

Provide a snapshot of the current suppliers and products available in the market place, to provide project stakeholders with confidence that there are potential solutions available to meet the project's requirements. Cross-reference the supplier name, supplier product and current price with the allocated product ID.

Table 3.37 Available products

Product ID	Supplier name	Supplier product	Price
CH1	ABC Ltd	Intel PC, including: • screen (19 inch monitor); • computer unit (latest Intel processor); • accessories (keyboard, mouse, CD reader).	$/£/other
RM1	DEF Ltd	Building construction materials, including: • wooden framing for walls; • roofing materials; • electrical cabling and switches.	$/£/other
CS1	XYZ Ltd	Consultancy services, including: • quality assurance auditing; • project office management; • accounting services.	$/£/other
...	...	...	...

Build a procurement schedule

Schedule

Schedule the activities required to select a preferred supplier, deliver the required products and review the supplier performance. See Figure 3.3 on the following page.

Assumptions

List any assumptions made during the procurement planning process. For example, it might be assumed that:

- the procurement requirements will not change;
- there will be no changes to market pricing;
- the pool of current suppliers will be available during the tender process.

Risks

List any risks identified during the procurement planning process. For example:

- the procurement requirements might not be defined in sufficient detail;
- the methods used to review supplier performance might not be adequate;
- the resource allocated to undertake supplier reviews might not be appropriately skilled.

3.10 CONTRACT THE SUPPLIERS

Having now created a suite of detailed plans for the project, the project manager will be ready to contract external suppliers to the project. While the procurement plan identifies the products to be procured from external suppliers, it does not describe in detail the method of selecting a preferred supplier with which to enter into a formal contract. This section covers the selection and appointment of a preferred supplier to the project.

The usual method of selecting a preferred supplier (or suppliers) is to undertake a formal tender management process. This is a method by which potential suppliers are identified, evaluated and selected for the provision of products (goods or services) to the project. This process involves creating a suite of tender documents which outline the project procurement requirements and information required from suppliers upon which to make a preferred supplier decision. The tender process is undertaken to ensure that the selection of preferred suppliers occurs in a fair and honest manner.

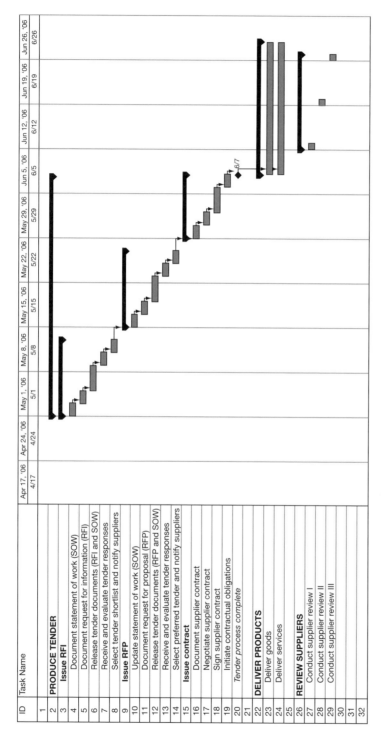

Figure 3.3 Detailed procurement schedule

Although a number of different types of tender management processes exist, this book provides a complete worked example of one particular type of tender management process called the RFI/RFP process. This process involves:

- issuing a statement of work (SOW) which describes the project requirements;
- issuing a request for information (RFI) which requests general supplier information;
- issuing a request for proposal (RFP) which requests detailed supplier proposals;
- receiving and evaluating supplier proposals;
- choosing a preferred supplier, based on merit;
- negotiating a formal contract with the preferred supplier.

This tender process should be undertaken whenever a product is required from outside the project and a preferred supplier has not yet been chosen. The process is initiated immediately after the procurement plan has been approved. It is usually undertaken by the project procurement manager. However, for large projects a tender committee may be formed to oversee the tender process.

Without a formal tender process in place, it may not be possible to show that the method by which preferred suppliers were selected was rigorous and fair. The tender process is terminated only when the preferred suppliers have been selected and the supplier contracts are formally signed.

Define the tender process

The first step towards contracting preferred suppliers is to define the process by which they will be selected. This section provides a complete worked example of an actual tender process to help you understand the steps necessary to appointing a preferred supplier.

Process overview

The purpose of the tender process is to provide a clear, robust and fair process for the appointment of preferred suppliers for the acquisition of product for the project. In summary, the tender process will be undertaken by the project through the implementation of three key processes:

- issue RFI;
- issue RFP;
- issue contract.

Figure 3.4 shows the processes and procedures required to select a preferred supplier for the project.

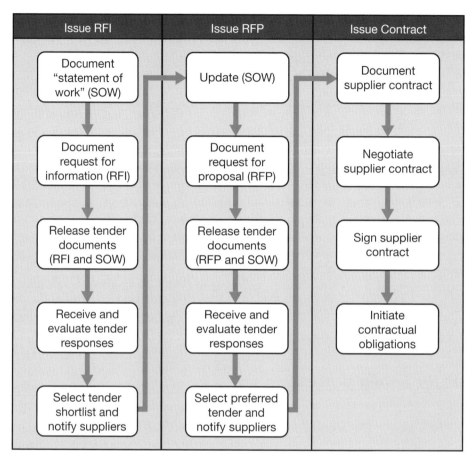

Figure 3.4 Tender management process

Issue RFI

The first step involves issuing an RFI to interested suppliers in the market place. The RFI requests that interested suppliers provide summary information describing their organization, the products they sell and their approach to procurement. The following procedures are undertaken:

Document a statement of work

A statement of work (SOW) will be documented to specify the procurement requirements of the project. The requirements will be defined in terms of the:

- supplier location, target market and experience;
- product types and quantity;

- training, documentation and support required;
- materials and equipment needed.

Document a request for information

Once the SOW has been defined, an RFI will be produced. The purpose of the RFI is to identify interested suppliers in the market place and find out basic information regarding their business and product offering. This information is then used to determine whether or not the supplier is likely to meet the requirements of the project as outlined in the SOW. The RFI will be documented by the project team and approved by the project manager.

Release tender documents (RFI and SOW)

The RFI and SOW are released to the market place to inform potential suppliers of the project requirement as outlined within the SOW and the format of the required response as outlined in the RFI. A set of explicit timeframes is provided for the supplier to formulate a response and send it to the project team for review.

Receive and evaluate tender responses

Once the response period has expired, the procurement manager (or officer) collates the responses received from interested suppliers and logs their details in the tender register. The tender responses are then formally evaluated. Responses are then rated and weighted according to predefined criteria.

Select tender short-list and notify suppliers

The responses with the highest scores are added to a tender short-list. Only short-listed suppliers will have the opportunity to take part in the next phase of the tender process, the RFP phase. Suppliers that are not on the short-list are formally notified that they will not be progressing to the next phase at that time.

Issue an RFP

The next tender process undertaken will be to issue a request for proposal (RFP) to the short-listed RFI suppliers. Short-listed suppliers respond to the RFP by providing a detailed proposal outlining their organization, the products they intend to provide and their approach to meeting the needs of the project. The following procedures are undertaken.

Update the SOW

Based on the responses to the RFI, the project team will have become more aware of the potential suppliers and products available in the market place, in addition to the information sourced already during the market research exercise. This information may be used to review the SOW and update the requirements, based on what is now thought available. For instance, a supplier may have suggested a new technology or approach previously not thought possible. Note that the team must be careful not to change the SOW based on only one supplier response, otherwise it could predetermine the overall result of the tender process.

Document a request for proposal

Once the SOW has been updated, an RFP is produced. The purpose of the RFP is to gather more detailed information from each supplier regarding the company, products and approach to the procurement requirement. This information is used to determine whether or not the supplier meets the detailed requirements set out in the SOW. The RFP is documented by the project team and approved by the project manager for release to the short-listed suppliers.

Release tender documents (RFP and updated SOW)

The RFP and updated SOW are released to the short-listed suppliers to inform them of the detailed project requirements and format for the response. As with the RFI process, the timeframe for receiving supplier responses will be made explicit.

Receive and evaluate tender responses

After the tender response period has expired, the procurement manager collates the responses received from the short-listed suppliers and enters their company details in the tender register. The tender responses are then formally evaluated, using more detailed criteria than that used during the RFI evaluation process.

Select preferred response and notify suppliers

The single response with the highest score is then selected as the preferred supplier and asked to enter the contract negotiation phase. All other suppliers are formally notified that they will not be progressing to the next phase. Note that while it is usual to have only one preferred supplier, it is possible to choose two or more preferred suppliers if they can meet the particular needs of the project.

Issue contract

The final phase of the tender process is the negotiation of the supplier contract. The contract forms the basis of the relationship, and specifies the terms and conditions surrounding the delivery of the product to the project. The following procedures are undertaken:

Document supplier contract

A formal supplier contract is drafted by the project team for the delivery of the supplier's product.

Negotiate supplier contract

The procurement manager and supplier then negotiate conditions that they believe to be fair and reasonable, and a contract is drawn up for approval. At this point, legal advice is sought to ensure that the contract does not put the project at risk.

Sign supplier contract

The project manager and supplier representative authorize the contract through formal signature.

Initiate contractual obligations

The responsibilities, terms and conditions stated within the contract are initiated. The contract is filed and a process is initiated to oversee the delivery of the product by the supplier.

Tender roles

Procurement manager/officer

The procurement manager is responsible for managing the entire tender management process. This includes:

- creating the SOW, RFI and RFP documents;
- obtaining approval to release the SOW, RFI and RFP documents to potential suppliers;
- collating the tender responses and organizing a tender review committee if required;
- organizing the tender evaluation process and working with the project manager to ensure that the preferred supplier is chosen fairly;
- notifying unsuccessful candidates that they will not be progressing further;
- documenting the draft supplier contract and leading supplier negotiations;
- finalizing the supplier contract and ensuring that legal council has been sought;
- keeping the tender register up to date at all times.

Project manager

The project manager acts as a checkpoint to ensure that the tender management process is undertaken efficiently and fairly by:

- approving the SOW, RFI and RFP tender documentation prior to its release;
- managing the tender evaluation process and approving the preferred supplier selection;
- resolving contractual negotiation issues and authorizing the final supplier contract.

Tender documents

The following tender documents are created:

- statement of work;
- request for information;
- request for proposal;
- supplier contract;
- tender register.

Issue a statement of work

Having now defined the tender management process, you will be ready to take the first step by formulating a SOW. The SOW defines the procurement requirements of the project in sufficient detail to enable potential suppliers to determine if they are able to meet those requirements. It is critical to the tender process that you clearly outline the procurement requirements within the SOW using simple terminology. If this is not achieved, it is less likely that the procurement requirements of the project will be fully satisfied, placing the project at risk.

The SOW is the first document created as part of the tender management process. It forms the basis upon which the tender documents (RFI, RFP) are formed, and is the core document against which supplier responses are evaluated. The SOW is written by the procurement manager and approved by the project manager. It is released to potential suppliers along with the tender documents, and updated throughout the tender process. This section describes in detail how to create a comprehensive SOW for release to potential suppliers in the market place.

Requirements

First, provide a brief summary of the project describing the objectives, scope, deliverables and milestones. List the generic types of product to be sourced from outside the project and the reasons they need to be sourced. Then list the requirements to be met by suppliers in order for them to become a preferred supplier for the project. Examples include:

- company requirements such as the size of the supplier, the industry within which it operates and its current target market;
- product requirements such as the types of products the supplier should offer and the number of years that the supplier should have been providing those products to the market place;
- training requirements such as the type and level of training offered by the supplier for the products produced;
- documentation requirements such as the type, depth and coverage of documentation offered by the supplier for the products produced;

- support requirements such as the type, hours and response times of operational support offered by the supplier for the products produced.

To help you create a comprehensive procurement requirements listing for your project, a suite of tables and worked examples is provided in the sections below.

Company requirements

List the requirements of the supplier company and the reasons these requirements are important to the project, by completing Table 3.38.

Table 3.38   Supplier requirements

Requirement	Reason
The supplier must have a minimum of five years trading in the relevant market segment.	It is important that the supplier organization is well established in the market place and is not likely to cease trading during the life of this project.
The supplier must operate in the computer sales market in the USA.	The supplier must currently be operating in a relevant local market segment.
The supplier must have provided the products to at least three customers who are able to act as reference sites within the last two years.	Proven delivery to other similar customers is critical to ensuring that the supplier has a valid supply chain.
...	...

Product requirements

Provide a detailed description of the specific products to be provided by the supplier, by completing Table 3.39.

Table 3.39 Product requirements

Product ID	Product	Description	Quantity
CH1	Computer hardware	Latest specification computer Intel PC, • screen (19 inch monitor) • computer unit (latest Intel processor); • accessories (keyboard, mouse); • latest Windows operating system; • MS Office software suite.	Number
CS1	Consultancy services	General consultancy services to assist with the management of the project, including: • quality assurance and auditing; • project office management; • accounting services.	Number
...	...	...	...

Note that a product ID has been assigned to each product listed, to allow you to link the product information between tables in this section.

Training requirements

List the training requirements for each product, by completing Table 3.40.

Table 3.40 Training requirements

Product ID	Training required?	Training description	No. trainees
CH1	Y	All end-users must be proficient in the use of the Windows operating system and MS Office software suite by the end of the course. Users must be able to operate the software to an *intermediate* level, thereby enabling them to undertake their roles efficiently. Two users must be able to operate the deployed software to an *advanced* level to enable them to problem solve and train other new users on an ongoing basis once the project has been completed.	Number
...	...	...	...

Documentation requirements

List the documentation required for each product, by completing Table 3.41.

Table 3.41 Documentation requirements

Product ID	Documentation required?	Documentation description
CH1	Y	The following documentation is required: • operating manual describing how to configure the software; • user manual describing how to use the software; • technical manual describing how to solve basic problems; • support procedures describing who to contact for support.
CS1	Y	The following documentation is required: • quality assurance audit report for each audit undertaken; • project office procedures, standards, guidelines and policies; • monthly balance sheet, profit and loss statement and cash-flow reports.
...	...	...

Support requirements

Describe the level of support required for each product, by completing Table 3.42.

Table 3.42 Support requirements

Product ID	Support required?	Support description
CH1	Y	The following level of support is required: • 24-hour call centre support to respond to end-user enquiries (1st level support); • 24-hour technical support to respond to end-user problems (2nd level support); • 8-hour working day support to resolve technology failures (3rd level support).
...	...	...

Materials and equipment

Compose a detailed list of the materials and equipment to be provided by the supplier.

Table 3.43   Equipment requirements

Product ID	Equipment	Materials
CH1	The following equipment is required: • deployment hardware; • training facilities; • support facilities.	The following materials are required: • deployment procedures; • training course notes; • support procedures.
CS1	The following equipment is required: • PC hardware and software; • project office facilities; • accounting system.	The following materials are required: • quality assurance audit procedures; • office stationery.
…	…	…

Schedule

Create a supplier delivery schedule listing the products, the date each product should be delivered to the project and the resource responsible for approving its delivery.

Table 3.44   Supplier delivery schedule

Product ID	Product	Due date	Approver
CH1	Computer hardware	xx/yy/zz	Procurement manager
CS1	Consultancy services	xx/yy/zz	Procurement manager
…	…	…	…

Acceptance

Outline the procedures for granting acceptance of the deliverables to the project, thereby authorizing supplier payment. Examples of procedures used in a SOW include:

- All products provided by the supplier must be reviewed and approved by the delegated project approver prior to supplier payment.

- Each product supplied must meet the requirements outlined within this SOW.
- Each product must have been provided to the project on or prior to the due date listed within this SOW.

Payments

Identify the conditions under which payment will be made for products provided by a supplier. Examples of payment conditions listed in a SOW include:

- Supplier invoices must have been received for products which have gained formal acceptance by the project approver.
- Invoices will be submitted monthly by the supplier and payment should be expected by the 20th of the month following the date of invoice.
- Invoices should be dated on the last day of the month for which the product was supplied.

Confidentiality

Specify whether or not a non-disclosure agreement (NDA) must be signed by the preferred supplier to ensure that sensitive information is handled in a professional and confidential manner. If an NDA is not required, describe in this section how sensitive project information relating to this tender should be handled. An example follows:

> During the course of this tender process, you may acquire confidential information relating to our business, project and/or customers. You agree to keep this information strictly confidential at all times, even after the project has been completed. You will not use it for your personal gain or the gain of any other person. You may disclose confidential information only to the extent that such disclosure is necessary for the submission of a formal supplier proposal. This does not apply to information that must legally be disclosed, or becomes available to and known by the public.

You are now ready to collate all of the materials listed in this section and create your statement of work document. The next step in the project life cycle is to issue an RFI.

Issue a request for information

An RFI is a document which is issued by a project to a wide group of potential suppliers to enable them to describe how they will meet the procurement requirements of the project, as documented in the SOW. The RFI requests that the suppliers provide summarized information regarding their:

- company size, industry;
- offering, products, training, documentation, support;
- approach, timeframes, pricing.

The RFI is issued along with the SOW to enable interested suppliers to understand the procurement requirements and provide them with the means of registering formal interest in the supply of product to the project. After issuing the RFI, a supplier short-list is selected by the project team. The short-listed suppliers are then provided with an RFP tender document, which requests a detailed proposal from each supplier, describing how it intends to meet the procurement needs of the project.

The RFP is very similar to the RFI. The key differentiator is that the RFI requires *summarized* information from each supplier to select a short-list of potential suppliers, whereas the RFP requires a *detailed* proposal from each supplier to enable the project team to select a preferred supplier. In some instances (especially for small projects) it may only be necessary to issue an RFI to select a preferred supplier. However in most cases a detailed proposal is required through the RFP process to make the preferred supplier decision.

The following sections list and describe the components of an RFI, giving real-life examples where appropriate.

Introduction

This section provides the supplier with an overview of the purpose of the RFI and the general tender process.

Purpose

Describe the purpose of the RFI document. For example:

> The purpose of this document is to inform interested suppliers of the information required to enable the project team to select a short-list of suppliers that could potentially fulfil the procurement needs of their project.

Acknowledgement

It is necessary for the receiver of the RFI document (the potential supplier) to acknowledge that it has received it to avoid any later disputes. List the instructions for the supplier to complete the acknowledgement process as follows:

> Please acknowledge that you have received this document by sending a formal written letter of receipt to the contact within the project team, at the following address:
>
> [Contact Name]
> [Street Address]
> [City]
> [Country]
>
> If you do not formally acknowledge the receipt of this document within 10 working days of the issue date, we will not be able to review any subsequent supplier submission.

Recipients

It is important to identify the general recipient group to whom the RFI will be sent, as each recipient will want to understand the level of competition for the tender when responding. For example:

> This tender document has been dispatched to all interested suppliers in the US computer and consumables market.

While it is usual to identify the type of supplier group to which the tender document will be released, it is not usual to identify any particular supplier company names for commercial confidentiality reasons.

Process

Describe the remaining tender process activities and provide the timeframes for each. For example:

> The tender process will be undertaken as follows. This RFI will be released to a particular market segment of potential suppliers. Suppliers must acknowledge receipt of the tender documentation and prepare a formal supplier response to be sent to the delegated contact within the project team. The project team will then review the supplier response against a set of predefined criteria and rate the response on its ability to satisfy the generic requirements stated in the SOW. A short-list of potential suppliers will be selected (with the highest awarded ratings) and formally notified. The short-listed suppliers will then be invited to take part in the RFP process, whereby they provide detailed information relating to the tender in a formal proposal. Supplier proposals will then be evaluated and a preferred supplier chosen. A formal contract will be negotiated with the preferred supplier and, if endorsed, the supplier will begin supplying the requisite product to the project. The following timeframes will be adhered to during this process:
>
> - Release tender documentation (RFI and SOW)   xx/yy/zz.
> - Closure date for receipt acknowledgements   xx/yy/zz.
> - Closure date for supplier responses   xx/yy/zz.
> - Review of supplier responses completed   xx/yy/zz.
> - Short-listed suppliers notified   xx/yy/zz.
> - Unsuccessful suppliers notified   xx/yy/zz.
> - Begin RFP process   xx/yy/zz.

Rules

List any rules which must be adhered to, in order to ensure that the supplier response is complete and accurate. Examples include:

- The supplier response must be accurate at the time of print and remain valid for the remainder of the tender process.

- Suppliers may work together to formulate one joint response. However the full details of each company must be included in the supplier response.
- The supplier must keep all tender information strictly confidential at all times.
- Formal supplier responses should be sent to the following address:
    [Contact name]
    [Street address]
    [City]
    [Country].

Questions

Identify the method of allowing suppliers to ask questions and receive answers about the tender process and timeframes.

Company

This section allows suppliers to describe their company background. Request that they provide the following information:

- vision, objectives;
- size, location;
- number of years in operation;
- number of customers;
- general products offered;
- market segments operating within;
- level of knowledge of industry;
- level of knowledge of products offered;
- level of expertise in products offered.

Offering

This section allows the supplier to describe their product (goods and/or services) offering, as relevant to the SOW.

Products

List the information required to provide the project team with an understanding of the products offered by the supplier. Examples include the:

- product name;
- product description;
- product activities (if a service);
- product purpose (its use);
- product capabilities;
- product quality.

Training

List the information required to provide the project team with an understanding of the training offered by the supplier. Examples include the:

- products for which training is offered;
- methods of training available (such as one-to-one, classroom, train-the-trainer);
- level of training available (such as beginner / intermediate / senior).

Documentation

List the information required to provide the project team with an understanding of the documentation offered by the supplier. Examples include the:

- products for which documentation is available;
- types of documents available;
- purpose of each document available.

Support

List the information required to provide the project team with an understanding of the support offered by the supplier. Examples include the:

- products for which support is available;
- types of support offered (such as first-, second- and third-level support);
- hours of support available.

Approach

This section allows suppliers to outline their intended implementation approach.

Method

List the information required to provide the project team with an understanding of the method of product delivery. The following information may be required:

- the method to be used for delivering the products to the project;
- the activities involved with training, documentation and support of the products.

Timeframes

List the information required to provide the project team with an understanding of the timeframes offered by the supplier for the delivery of the products. The following information may be required:

- approximate lead times on sourcing each product;
- approximate length of time required to deliver each product (from order request to order completion).

Pricing

List the information required to provide the project team with an understanding of the product pricing proposed by the supplier. The following information may be required:

- price of each set of related products in bulk;
- price of other offerings;
- any other applicable costs such as tax, freight, administration charges.

Other

This section allows the project team to request any other information deemed necessary to the tender process.

Confidentiality

It may be necessary to request that the supplier explicitly agrees to the confidentiality statements outlined in the SOW. For clarity, we suggest you repeat those statements here:

- During the course of this tender process, you may acquire confidential information relating to our business, project and/or customers.
- You agree to keep this information strictly confidential at all times, even after the project has been completed.
- You will not use it for your personal gain or the gain of any other person.
- You may disclose confidential information only to the extent that such disclosure is necessary for the submission of a formal supplier proposal.
- This does not apply to information that must legally be disclosed, or that becomes available to and known by the public.

Note: if any suppliers do not agree with these clauses, they should explicitly state this in their response.

Documentation

List any other information required to provide the project team with the confidence that the supplier can meet the generic procurement requirements stated in the SOW. Examples of other documentation requested include:

- product specifications or marketing brochures;
- website addresses for product listings;
- profiles of staff providing services.

You are now ready to collate all of the materials listed in this section and create your RFI document. The next step in the project life cycle is to issue an RFP.

Issue a request for proposal

An RFP is a document which is issued by a project team to a short-listed group of suppliers to enable them to define in detail how they will meet the procurement requirements outlined in the SOW. The RFP requests that the suppliers provide detailed information regarding the:

- company size and industry;
- solution type and its components;
- training offered for solution;
- documentation provided with solution;
- support available for solution;
- implementation schedule and method;
- pricing structure for each product.

The RFP is issued immediately after the RFI process has been undertaken and a short-list of potential suppliers has been selected. The RFP is very similar to the RFI. The key differentiator is that the RFI requires *summarized* information from each supplier to select a short-list of potential suppliers, whereas the RFP requires a *detailed* proposal from each supplier to enable the project team to select a preferred supplier.

   The RFP is typically written by the procurement manager and approved by the project manager. It is released to short-listed suppliers along with the SOW, which defines in detail the project's procurement requirements. The following sections list the actual components of an RFP and provide real-life examples where appropriate.

Introduction

This section describes the purpose of the RFP document and outlines the procedural requirements for the submission of supplier proposals to the project team.

Purpose

Describe the purpose of the RFP document. For example:

> The purpose of this document is to inform short-listed suppliers of the detailed information required (in the form of a proposal) to enable the project team to select a preferred supplier.

Acknowledgement

It is generally necessary for the receiver of the RFP document (the supplier) to acknowledge that it has received the document. List the instructions for the supplier to complete the acknowledgement process as follows:

Please acknowledge that you have received this document by sending a formal written letter of receipt to the contact within the project team, at the following address:

[Contact name]
[Street address]
[City]
[Country]

If you do not formally acknowledge the receipt of this document within 10 working days of the issue date, we will not be able to review any subsequent supplier submissions.

Recipients

It is important to identify the general recipient group to whom the RFP will be sent, as each recipient will want to understand the level of competition for the tender when responding. For example:

This tender document has been dispatched to a short-listed group of three potential suppliers within the US market.

Note that while it is usual to identify the type of supplier group to which the tender document will be released, it is not usual to identify any particular supplier company names for commercial confidentiality reasons.

Process

Identify the remaining activities in the tender process and allocate timeframes to each activity listed. For example:

The tender process will be undertaken as follows. This RFP will be released to a short-list of potential suppliers. Suppliers must acknowledge receipt of the tender documentation and prepare a formal supplier proposal to be sent to the delegated contact within the project team. The project team will then review the supplier proposals against a set of predefined criteria and rate each proposal on its ability to satisfy the requirements stated in the SOW. A preferred supplier will be chosen (with the highest awarded rating) and formally notified. A formal contract will be negotiated with the preferred supplier and, if endorsed, the supplier then will begin supplying the requisite product to the project. The following time-frames will be adhered to during this process:

* Release tender documentation (RFP and SOW)   xx/yy/zz.
* Closure date for receipt acknowledgements   xx/yy/zz.
* Closure date for supplier proposals   xx/yy/zz.
* Review of supplier proposals complete   xx/yy/zz.
* Preferred supplier notified   xx/yy/zz.
* Unsuccessful suppliers notified   xx/yy/zz.

- Draft supplier contract drawn up   xx/yy/zz.
- Supplier contract signed   xx/yy/zz.
- Supplier contract initiated   xx/yy/zz.

Rules

List any rules which must be adhered to, in order to ensure that the supplier response is complete and accurate. For example:

- The supplier response must be accurate at the time of print and remain valid for the remainder of the tender process.
- Suppliers may work together to formulate one joint response. However, the full details of each company must be included in the supplier response.
- The supplier must keep all tender information confidential at all times.
- Formal supplier responses should be sent to the following address:
  [Contact name]
  [Street address]
  [City]
  [Country].

Questions

Identify the method of allowing suppliers to ask questions and receive answers about the tender process and timeframes.

Company

This section allows suppliers to describe in detail the relevant aspects of their company.

Background

List the information required to provide the project team with a detailed understanding of the company. The following information may be required:

- vision, objectives;
- size, location;
- number of years in operation;
- number of customers;
- location of customers;
- length of customer relationships;
- customer reference sites.

Offering

List the information required to provide the project team with a detailed understanding of the company offering. The following information may be required:

- general products offered (including goods and services);
- target market within which the products are sold;
- market share currently held by the supplier;
- number of competitors and their product offerings.

Experience

List the information required to provide the project team with a detailed understanding of the experience of the company. The following information may be required:

- number of years selling product within each market segment;
- average number of years each staff member has been with the company;
- level of industry knowledge and experience;
- level of product knowledge and experience.

Solution

This section allows suppliers to describe their proposed solution. This solution will involve the supply of one or more products as well as a range of other offerings including training, documentation and support which are customized to meet the requirements of the SOW.

Products

List the information required to provide the project team with a detailed understanding of the specific products proposed as part of the overall solution. The following information may be required:

- product name;
- product description;
- product components (if a 'good');
- product activities (if a 'service');
- product quantity (the number of each particular product proposed);
- product purpose (its use);
- product capabilities;
- product quality.

Note that as the products section is the most critical section in the RFP, it is important to stress to suppliers that *detailed* information is required for this section to gain a full appreciation of the solution being offered.

Training

List the information required to provide the project team with a detailed understanding of the training offered by the supplier. The following information may be required:

- products for which training is required;
- method of training proposed (such as one-to-one, classroom, train-the-trainer);
- level of training to be given (such as beginner/intermediate/senior);
- number of trainees to be given training.

Documentation

List the information required to provide the project team with a detailed understanding of the documentation offered by the supplier. The following information may be required:

- products for which documentation will be provided;
- actual documents to be generated;
- purpose of each document provided;
- depth of each document provided;
- target audience for each document provided.

Support

List the information required to provide the project team with a detailed understanding of the support offered by the supplier. The following information may be required:

- products for which support is provided;
- types of support provided (such as first-, second-, third-level support);
- response times for support provided;
- hours for support provided;
- organizations involved in providing support.

Implementation

This section allows suppliers to describe their proposed implementation approach. This includes the methods of deploying the requisite products as well as the time-frames for delivery.

Approach

List the information required to provide the project team with a detailed understanding of the approach to be taken by the supplier towards deployment of the products and other deliverables. The following information may be required:

- the method for delivery of the products listed;
- the activities involved with training, documentation and support;
- the activities involved with undertaking other project deliverables.

Timeframes

List the information required to provide the project team with a detailed understanding of the timeframes proposed by the supplier for the delivery of the solution. The following information may be required:

- likely start and end dates for the delivery of each product and other deliverables proposed within the solution;
- the date the product must be ordered by to ensure that it is dispatched within the timeframes required.

Pricing

List the information required to provide the project team with a detailed understanding of the pricing proposed by the supplier for the delivery of the solution. The following information may be required:

- price of each product and its components per unit;
- price of each set of related products and any bulk discount applied;
- price of other items such as training, documentation and support;
- any other applicable costs (such as tax, freight, administration charges).

Other

This section allows the project team to request any other information deemed necessary to the tender process.

Confidentiality

It may be necessary to request that suppliers explicitly agree to the confidentiality statements outlined in the SOW, if they have not already done so. For clarity, we suggest you repeat those statements here:

- During the course of this tender process, you may acquire confidential information relating to our business, project and/or customers.
- You agree to keep this information strictly confidential at all times, even after the project has been completed.
- You will not use it for your personal gain or the gain of any other person.
- You may disclose confidential information only to the extent that such disclosure is necessary for the submission of a formal supplier proposal.
- This does not apply to information that must legally be disclosed, or that becomes available to and known by the public.

Note that if suppliers do not agree with these clauses, they should explicitly state this in their response.

Documentation

List any other information required to provide the project team with confidence that the supplier can meet the requirements stated in the SOW. Examples include:

- product specifications or marketing brochures;
- website addresses for further product information;
- profiles of staff offering to provide services.

You are now ready to collate all the materials listed in this section and create your request for proposal (RFP) document. Following the release of the RFP and selection of a preferred supplier, the next step in the project life cycle is to formalize the relationship with the supplier by creating a supplier contract.

Negotiate supplier contracts

A supplier contract is an agreement between the project team ('Project') and an external supply company ('Supplier') for the acquisition of a defined set of products to meet the procurement requirements of the project. The supplier contract is a legal document which is used as the basis upon which to make supplier payments during the procurement cycle. The contract specifically defines the:

- products (goods and services) to be provided by the supplier;
- responsibilities of the project and supplier in acquiring the products;
- contract review points to assess performance;
- price of each product acquired;
- invoicing and payments processes;
- terms and conditions applicable.

A supplier contract should be used whenever a formal agreement is required between the project and a preferred supplier for the acquisition of product. A supplier contract is usually documented in the last phase of the tender process, after the RFP supplier proposals have been received and a preferred supplier has been appointed. Following the endorsement of the supplier contract, a procurement management process is initiated to monitor and control the supply of product to the project.

The supplier contract is typically written by the procurement manager and approved by the project manager or sponsor. Without a formal supplier contract in place, it will be more difficult to manage legally the performance of the supplier. A clearly written supplier contract will reduce performance management issues by specifying the deliverables and responsibilities of both parties to ensure that the product procurement takes place efficiently.

The following sections list the components of a supplier contract and provide real-life examples where appropriate.

Introduction

The first section in a supplier contract describes the purpose of the contract and provides clear definitions for frequently used terminology.

Purpose

Describe the purpose of the supplier contract. For example:

> The purpose of this document is to clearly outline the responsibilities of both the supplier and project team in meeting the requirements laid down by the statement of work (SOW).

Recipients

It is important to identify the recipient group who will receive copies of this supplier contract. By signing and receiving a copy of this contract, they thereby initiate their obligations under the contract.

Definitions

Provide definitions for the key words used in the document that potentially have ambiguous meanings, by completing Table 3.45.

Table 3.45 Contract definitions

Term	Definition
Supplier	*<Supplier company name>*, a duly incorporated company with the head office based in *<Supplier address>*.
Project	*<Project>*, a formally established project owned by *<organization name>* based in *<organization address>*.
Deliverables	'Deliverables' are a suite of products and other items (such as training, documentation and support) provided by the supplier to the project.
Products	'Products' are goods and services provided by the supplier to the project, as listed in the following section.
General	Words used in singular shall include the plural definition and vice versa.
...	...

Deliverables

This section clearly outlines the deliverables to be produced by the supplier to meet the full requirements of the SOW.

Products

List the products to be provided by the supplier to the project team and for each, describe the product:

- name;
- description;
- components (if a 'good');
- activities (if a 'service');
- quantity (the number of each product);
- purpose (its usage);
- capabilities;
- quality.

Note that as this is the most critical section in the supplier contract, it is important to stress that *specific* information must be provided to ensure that the product delivery requirements are clear and unambiguous.

Training

Identify the level of training to be provided by the supplier to the project team, by describing the:

- products for which training will be provided;
- method of training (such as one-to-one, classroom, train-the-trainer);
- level of training to be provided (such as beginner/intermediate/senior);
- number of trainees to be given training.

Documentation

List the documentation to be provided by the supplier to the project team, by describing the:

- products for which documentation will be provided;
- actual documents to be generated;
- depth of each document provided;
- target audience for each document provided.

Support

Describe the level of support to be provided by the supplier, by describing the:

- products for which support will be provided;
- type of support (such as first-, second-, third-level support);
- response times for support provided;
- hours for support provided;
- organizations involved in providing support.

Schedule

Provide a detailed schedule highlighting the timeframes for delivering products to the project. See Figure 3.5 on the following page.

Responsibilities

This section describes the responsibilities of the supplier and the project in producing and receiving the required products.

Supplier

List the responsibilities of the supplier. For instance, it might be responsible for:

- supplying the product for review and acceptance by the project team;
- supplying product which meets the procurement requirements listed in the SOW;
- notifying the project team if there are likely to be delivery issues resulting in a delay;
- informing the project team if there are likely to be any changes to the product supplied.

Project

List the responsibilities of the project team. For instance, it might be responsible for:

- formally notifying the supplier of the receipt of each product;
- reviewing each product against the procurement requirements listed in the SOW;
- formally notifying the supplier of the acceptance of each product;
- informing the supplier of required changes to the product.

Performance

This section describes how the supplier's performance will be reviewed during the procurement process.

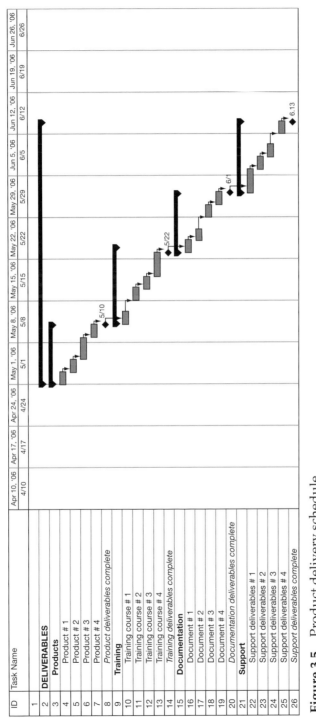

Figure 3.5 Product delivery schedule

Criteria

List the criteria against which the performance of the supplier will be assessed, using Table 3.46.

Table 3.46 Supplier review criteria

Criterion	Description
Completeness	The ability of the supplier to deliver the complete set of products listed in this contract. Each product must be provided in its entirety without compromise.
Quality	The ability of the supplier to deliver the level of quality of products, as defined in the SOW.
Quantity	The ability of the supplier to deliver the total quantity of products, as defined in the SOW.
Timeliness	The ability of the supplier to deliver the products within the timeframes listed in this contract.
...	...

Reviews

Outline the process and schedule for reviewing supplier performance throughout the execution of the contract. For example:

The process by which supplier performance will be reviewed is as follows:

- The project team will review all products delivered to date to determine whether or not they meet the performance criteria defined by this contract. The project team will also assess whether the terms and conditions of this contract have been fully complied with.
- If the project team identifies a deviation between the terms of this contract and the actual supplier's performance, a formal issue will be raised within the project team and discussions will commence with the supplier to identify an appropriate resolution.
- If a resolution is not possible, a formal dispute will be raised.
- The supplier will be notified of the outcome of the review within five working days of the completion of the review.

Figure 3.6 provides a basic example of a supplier review schedule.

ID	Task Name	Dec 8, '03 12/8	Dec 15, '03 12/15	Dec 22, '03 12/22	Dec 29, '03 12/29	Jan 5, '03 1/5	Jan 12, '03 1/12	Jan 19, '03 1/19	Jan 26, '03 1/26
1									
2	**REVIEWS**								
3	**Supplier performance review # 1**								
4	Assess supplier performance								
5	Document supplier performance								
6	Resolve performance issues							1/23	
7	*Review # 1 complete*								
8	**Supplier performance review # 2**								
9	Assess supplier performance								
10	Document supplier performance								
11	Resolve performance issues							1/23	
12	*Review # 2 complete*								
13	**Supplier performance review # 3**								
14	Assess supplier performance								
15	Document supplier performance								
16	Resolve performance issues							1/23	
17	*Review # 3 complete*								
18									

Figure 3.6 Supplier review schedule

Pricing

This section identifies the price to be paid for each deliverable provided by the supplier. The invoicing and payments process is also outlined.

Schedule

List each of the deliverables and their respective prices in Table 3.47.

Table 3.47 Contract delivery schedule

Deliverable	Price per unit	Total price
Products Product #1 Product #2 …	*$ / £ / other currency*	
Training Training course #1 Training course #2 …		
Documentation Document #1 Document #2 …		
Support Support method #1 Support method #2 …		
…	…	…

Describe the conditions that trigger a supplier payment, such as the end of the month in which the products were delivered or the completion of a major project milestone or activity.

Invoicing

Describe the process to be undertaken to issue and approve supplier invoices for payment. For example:

- Invoices will be generated for deliverables received and accepted by the project.
- Invoices will be submitted by the supplier and paid by the 20th of the following month.
- Invoices will be dated on the last day of the month within which they were produced.
- In the event of an invoice being disputed, the project team shall pay the undisputed portion of the invoice and the amount in dispute shall be dealt with separately.

Terms and conditions

This section lists the terms and conditions required to administer the contract.

Confidential information

Identify how sensitive project information relating to this contract should be handled by the supplier. An example follows:

> During the course of this contract, you may acquire confidential information relating to our business, project and/or customers. You agree to keep this information strictly confidential at all times, even after the project has been completed. You will not use or attempt to use it for your personal gain or the gain of any other person. You may disclose confidential information only to the extent that such disclosure is necessary for the execution of your responsibilities under this contract. This does not apply to information that must legally be disclosed or that becomes available to and known by the public.

Termination

List the conditions and process for allowing either party to terminate the contract. For example:

> This contract may be terminated by either party after 30 days written notice. At that time, all supplier invoices up to the date of termination should be paid for, unless a dispute has been formally raised by the project team with the supplier. Upon termination, the project team and supplier will be released from all responsibilities provided by this contract.

Disputes

Describe the process undertaken to raise a dispute under the contract. For example:

> If an issue cannot be resolved through direct negotiation between the supplier and the project team, a formal 'dispute' must be raised and the other party notified of the dispute in writing. The matter in dispute shall be referred to and settled by *<arbitrator company>* or *<association name>*. The decision of the arbitrator is final and shall be binding on both parties. Following the resolution of the dispute, both parties shall continue to undertake their responsibilities under this contract as if the dispute had not occurred.

Indemnity

Include any indemnity clauses required by either party to the contract. An indemnity clause provides a party with legal exemption from damage, loss or injury caused to the other party. Furthermore, it negates or limits the possible compensation claimed for damage, loss or injury suffered by the other party.

Law

Identify the country for which legislation will govern the contract. For example:

> The legislation of the United States of America (USA) shall govern this contract. Both parties consent to the jurisdiction of the US courts.

Agreement

Add the following statement:

> This contract constitutes the entire contract between both parties and it supersedes all other contracts, agreements or understandings previously or currently in existence. Only changes authorized in writing shall constitute a modification to this contract.

You are now ready to collate all of the materials listed in this section and create your supplier contract document. After the project team and the supplier approve the supplier contract, the final step in the planning phase is to perform a phase review.

3.11 PERFORM A PHASE REVIEW

At the end of the planning phase, a phase review is performed. This is a checkpoint to ensure that the project has achieved its stated objectives as planned. A phase review form is completed to formally request approval to proceed to the next phase of a project. The form should describe the status of the:

- overall project;
- project schedule based on the project plan;
- project expenses based on the financial plan;
- project staffing based on the resource plan;
- project deliverables based on the quality plan;
- project risks based on the risk register;
- project issues based on the issues register.

The review form should be completed by the project manager and approved by the project sponsor. To obtain approval, the project manager will usually present the current status of the project to the project board for consideration. The project board (chaired by the project sponsor) may decide to cancel the project, undertake further work within the existing project phase or grant approval to begin the next phase of the project.

A phase review form for the project planning phase is shown as Figure 3.7.

PROJECT DETAILS	
Project name:	Report prepared by:
Project manager:	Report preparation date:
Project sponsor:	Reporting period:

Project description:
[Summarize the overall project achievements, risks and issues experienced to date.]

OVERALL STATUS

Overall status: *[Description]*
Project schedule: *[Description]*
Project expenses: *[Description]*
Project deliverables: *[Description]*
Project risks: *[Description]*
Project issues: *[Description]*
Project changes: *[Description]*

REVIEW DETAILS

Review category	Review question	Answer	Variance
Schedule	Was the phase completed to schedule?	[Y/N]	
Expenses	Was the phase completed within budgeted cost?	[Y/N]	
Deliverables:			
Project plan	Was a project plan approved?	[Y/N]	
Resource plan	Was a resource plan approved?	[Y/N]	
Financial plan	Was a financial plan approved?	[Y/N]	
Quality plan	Was a quality plan approved?	[Y/N]	
Risk plan	Was a risk plan approved?	[Y/N]	
Acceptance plan	Was an acceptance plan approved?	[Y/N]	
Communications plan	Was a communications plan approved?	[Y/N]	
Procurement plan	Was a procurement plan approved?	[Y/N]	
Statement of work	Was a statement of work released?	[Y/N]	
Request for information	Was a request for information released?	[Y/N]	
Request for proposal	Was a request for proposal released?	[Y/N]	
Supplier contract	Was a supplier contract approved?	[Y/N]	
Risks	Are there any outstanding project risks?	[Y/N]	
Issues	Are there any outstanding project issues?	[Y/N]	
Changes	Are there any outstanding project changes?	[Y/N]	

Figure 3.7 Phase review form for the planning phase

APPROVAL DETAILS
Supporting documentation: *[Reference any supporting documentation used to substantiate the review details above.]*   **Project sponsor**   **Signature:** _____ **Date:** ___/___/___   This project is approved to proceed to the project execution phase.

Figure 3.7 *continued*

4

Project execution

4.1 INTRODUCTION

After you have carefully planned your project, you will be ready to start the project execution phase. The execution phase is typically the longest phase of the project. It is the phase within which the deliverables are physically built and presented to the customer for acceptance. To ensure that the customer's requirements are met, the project manager monitors and controls the production of each deliverable by executing a suite of management processes. After the deliverables have been physically constructed and accepted by the customer, a phase review is carried out to determine whether the project is complete and ready for closure. Figure 4.1 shows the activities undertaken during the project execution phase.

To successfully deliver the project on time, within budget and to specification you need to fully implement each of the activities listed in this section. Even though the management processes listed may seem obvious, it is extremely important that you implement each process in its entirety and that you communicate the process clearly to your project team. A large percentage of projects worldwide have failed because of a lack of formalization of these simple, yet critical project management processes.

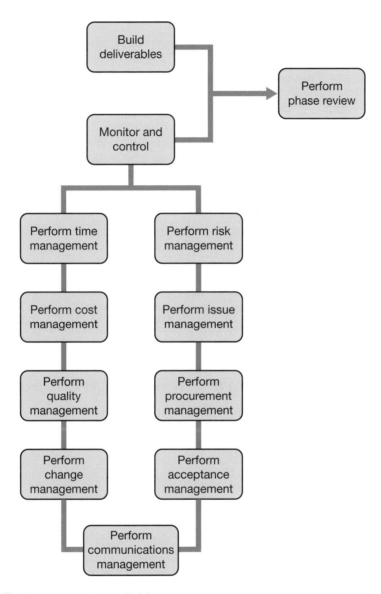

Figure 4.1 Project execution activities

4.2 BUILD DELIVERABLES

The most time-consuming activity in the project is the creation of the physical project deliverables. Whether you are building a new bridge, creating new computer software or implementing a new customer service offering, your project will consume the majority of its available resource building the actual deliverables for acceptance by the customer.

The steps undertaken to build each deliverable will vary depending on the type of project you are undertaking, and cannot therefore be described here in any real detail. For instance engineering and telecommunications projects will focus on using equipment, resources and materials to construct each project deliverable, whereas computer projects may require the development and implementation of software code routines to produce each project deliverable. The activities required to build each deliverable will be clearly specified within the terms of reference and project plan accordingly.

There are a variety of methods used to construct deliverables. For instance, deliverables may be constructed in a 'waterfall' fashion, where each activity is undertaken in sequence until the final deliverable has been completed. An alternative method is the iterative approach, whereby iterations of each deliverable are constructed until the final deliverable meets the requirements of the customer. Regardless of the method used to construct each deliverable, careful monitoring and control processes should be employed to ensure that the quality of the final deliverable meets the acceptance criteria set by the customer.

4.3 MONITOR AND CONTROL

While the project team are physically constructing each deliverable, the project manager undertakes a series of management processes to monitor and control the activities being undertaken. An overview of each management process follows.

4.4 PERFORM TIME MANAGEMENT

Time management process

The time management process is the method by which time spent by staff undertaking project tasks is recorded against the project. Recording the actual time spent by staff on a project has various purposes. It is used to:

- calculate the total time spent undertaking each task as well as the total staff cost of undertaking each task in the project;
- enable the project manager to control the level of resource allocated to each task;
- identify the percentage of each task completed as well as the amount of outstanding work required to complete each task in its entirety.

Time management is undertaken through the completion and approval of timesheets. A timesheet is a document which records an allocation of time against a set of project activities listed on the project plan. Timesheets are typically completed weekly, by all members of the project. This includes project staff, contractors and often suppliers. If timesheets are not recorded, then it may be difficult to accurately assess the amount of time spent undertaking project activities, and therefore become impossible to manage the project constraints of time, cost and quality.

Although the time management process is usually initiated after the project plan has been formally documented and the project is under way (in other words, during the execution phase of the project), timesheets may be completed at any phase of the project if requested by the project manager. For instance, it may be necessary to record timesheets throughout the entire project to ensure that the full costs of the project are captured.

Figure 4.2 shows the processes and procedures to be undertaken to document, approve and register timesheets within the project. Where applicable, time management roles have also been identified.

Document timesheet

This process involves the capture of information related to the time spent undertaking each task on the project. Time spent undertaking each task will be recorded for the entire duration of the completion of the task. Time should be recorded against all project tasks for the entire project execution phase. From the moment time is spent undertaking a project task, it should be recorded using a timesheet. Timesheets exist in various forms, including paper-based, spreadsheet and software-based formats. The most accurate method of capturing timesheet information is to request that all project staff record time in timesheets as they undertake each task, as opposed to waiting till the end of the reporting period before capturing the information.

Approve timesheet

Timesheets should be submitted by each member of the team to the project manager, for approval on a regular (for example, weekly) basis. Following the receipt of a timesheet, the project manager will:

- confirm that the tasks undertaken were valid tasks as listed in the project plan;
- confirm that the staff member was in fact a resource allocated to complete the task;
- decide if the outcome of the time spent is reasonable.

Based on the above information, the project manager will approve the timesheet, request further information from the staff member regarding the time spent, or decline the timesheet and raise a staff issue.

Register timesheet

The details of all approved timesheets are formally recorded in a timesheet register, enabling:

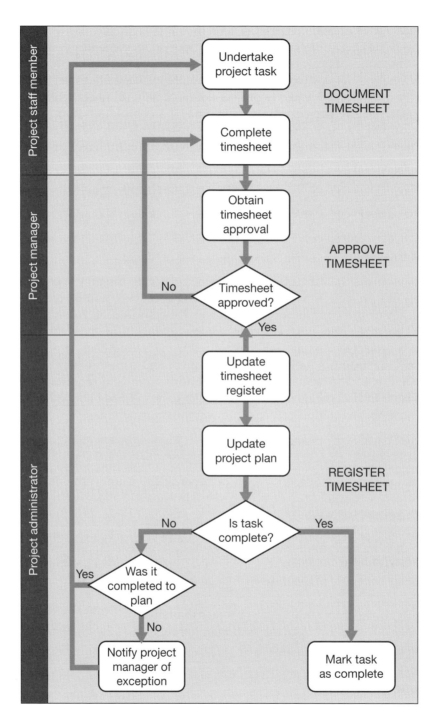

Figure 4.2 Time management process

- the project plan to be updated with a summary of the time recorded against each task;
- the cost of each staff member to be calculated and monitored throughout the project;
- the identification of overtime for the project.

On a regular basis, summarized timesheet information should be extracted from the timesheet register and entered into the project plan. This enables the project administrator to:

- produce a view of the overall progress of the project to date;
- forecast task slippage (that is, identify tasks that might not be completed by the due date);
- identify any exceptions (for example, instances where tasks have been completed using more time than had been allocated).

The project administrator then provides the project manager with a copy of the updated project plan and raises any areas of slippage or exception. It is then up to the project manager to take action based on the extent of the deviation from plan. Examples of actions taken include:

- changing the individual / amount of resource allocated to the task;
- allocating additional funds to complete the task;
- requesting assistance from an external supplier to complete the task;
- raising a project issue for action by the project board / sponsor.

Once tasks have been completed, they are marked in the timesheet register and project plan as 100 per cent complete. After a task has been marked as 100 per cent complete, no further time can be allocated against it for the duration of the project.

Time management roles

The following roles and responsibilities are involved with the management of time spent by staff within the project.

Project staff member

Project staff members are responsible for:

- undertaking each delegated task to the best of their ability;
- completing regular timesheets to the level of detail requested;
- submitting timesheets to the project manager as required;
- providing the project manager with further information regarding the time spent undertaking the task, if required.

Project manager

The project manager has overall responsibility for the time management process, including:

- delegating tasks to project staff members and providing them with the resources and support required to undertake each task effectively;
- ensuring that all staff are informed of the time management process, that they understand when timesheets need to be submitted, to whom and in how much detail;
- reviewing and approving all timesheets on the project;
- creating action plans to address deviations from plan;
- resolving all timesheet issues with staff members and raising any generic time-related issues to the project board / sponsor for action.

Project administrator

The project administrator manages the day-to-day timesheet process by:

- providing all staff with the basic timesheet template for completion;
- ensuring that all timesheets are completed on time and to the required level of detail;
- checking that all timesheets have been reviewed and approved by the project manager;
- obtaining further information from staff members, should it be requested by the project manager when reviewing timesheets for approval;
- loading the details of all approved timesheets into the timesheet register;
- entering the summarized timesheet register information into the project plan and identifying any slippage / exceptions for the project manager's attention.

Time management documents

Timesheet form

A timesheet is a document completed by project staff to formally record the time spent undertaking an activity or task. An example is shown as Table 4.1.

Timesheet register

The timesheet register is the central log where all timesheet information is formally recorded for the project. An example is shown as Table 4.2.

Table 4.1 Sample timesheet

TIMESHEET FORM

Project name: Name of the project for which time is allocated to
Project manager: Name of the project manager responsible for this project
Staff member: Name of the person entering time against the project

Date	Day	Activity	Task	Start time	End time	Duration	Start % complete	End % complete	Outcome
[xx/yy/zz]	Mon	[Activity description, as referenced in the project plan]	[Task description, as referenced in the project plan]	[xx:yy]	[xx:yy]	[x hrs]	[xx:yy]	[xx:yy]	[Result of time spent; eg 'Task complete and deliverable produced']
	Tue								
	Wed								
	Thu								
	Fri								
	Sat								
	Sun								

APPROVAL DETAILS

Submitted by

Name:

Signature: _____ Date: __ / __ / __

Approved by

Name:

Signature: _____ Date: __ / __ / __

PLEASE FORWARD THIS FORM TO THE PROJECT MANAGER FOR APPROVAL

Table 4.2   Sample timesheet register

TIMESHEET REGISTER
Project name:
Project manager:

Work undertaken				Time spent			Result achieved				Approval		
Activity ID	Activity description	Task ID	Task description	Staff member	Standard time	Over-time	Outcome	Start % complete	End % complete	Approval status	Approval date	Approver	

4.5 PERFORM COST MANAGEMENT

Cost management process

A cost management process is a method by which costs/expenses incurred on the project are formally identified, approved and paid. Examples of cost types are:

- labour costs (for staff, external suppliers, contractors and consultants);
- equipment costs (for example computers, furniture, building facilities, machinery and vehicles);
- material costs (such as stationery, consumables, building materials, water and power);
- administration costs (such as legal, insurance, lending and accounting fees).

The purpose of the cost management process is to accurately record the actual costs/ expenses which accrue during the project life cycle. Cost management is undertaken through the completion and approval of expense forms. An expense form is a document that is completed by a team member to request the payment of an expense which has already been incurred, or is about to be incurred, on the project. A single expense form may be completed for multiple expenses in the project. Regardless of the number of expenses incurred, payment will not be made to the payee until a completed expense form has been approved by the project manager. Each expense form must specify:

- the activity and tasks listed in the project plan against which the expense occurred;
- the date on which the expense occurred;
- the type of expense (for example labour, equipment, materials, administration);
- a detailed description of the expense;
- the amount of the expense claimed;
- the payee to whom payment should be made;
- the invoice number related to the expense (if applicable).

Expense forms should be completed for *all* project expenses, including contractor, supplier, equipment, materials and administration expenses. Staff salary expenses are exempt as total salary expenses can be calculated from the timesheet information provided to the project manager on a regular basis. Expense forms should be completed weekly and provided to the project manager for approval. Upon approval, the expense information is entered into an expense register to enable the project manager to track and record the physical costs of the project. Summarized expense information is also entered into the project plan to record the actual spend against the planned spend. Although expense forms are typically completed during the execution phase of the project, it may be requested that they be completed during any project phase to ensure that the full costs of the project are captured.

Figure 4.3 shows the processes and procedures to be undertaken to document, approve and register expenses within the project. Where applicable, cost management roles have also been identified:

Document expense

The first step involves the capture of information relating to an expense incurred on the project. Expenses are incurred on the project when undertaking project activities and tasks. It is therefore important to identify the project activity and task related to each expense incurred so that the total cost of undertaking project activities and tasks on the project can be calculated.

Expense forms should be completed regularly by:

- members of the project who have had to incur expenses;
- project administrators, on behalf of external suppliers who have issued invoices for goods and services rendered;
- contractors allocated to the project for services provided.

Approve expense

Completed expense forms should be forwarded to the project manager for review and approval. The project manager will consider whether:

- the tasks for which the expense occurred are valid, as listed in the project plan;
- the expense was originally budgeted, as defined in the financial plan;
- any unbudgeted expenditure is fair, reasonable and affordable.

The project manager may have authority to approve only budgeted expenditure. Unbudgeted expenditure over a certain limit may require the approval of the project board or sponsor. The project manager may then either:

- approve the expense and forward it to the project administrator for payment;
- request further information from the person submitting the form;
- decline the expense and raise an issue with the person submitting the form.

Following formal approval of the expense by the project manager, payment will be scheduled. It is typical to pay expenses in batches to reduce the administrative work-load in making expense payments and manage project cash-flow more effectively.

Register expense

After the payment has been scheduled, the expense register should be updated to ensure that an accurate record of the approval and payment is kept. Although the register must

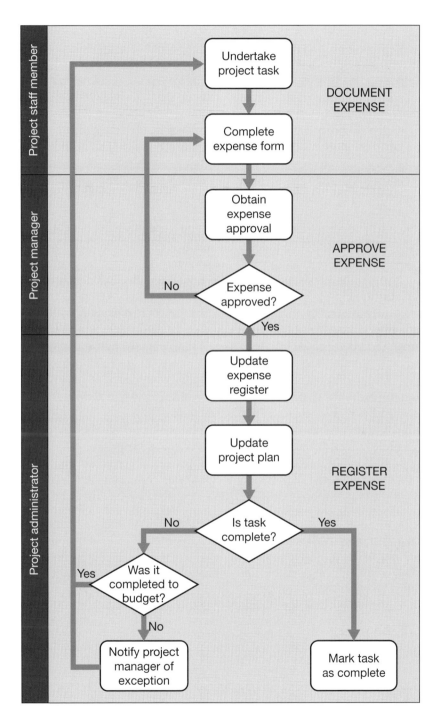

Figure 4.3   Cost management process

be updated after the expense has been approved, the register should be updated throughout the process to ensure that the project manager is kept informed of the expense status at all phases in the expense approval cycle.

The expense register records the full details of all expense forms submitted, thereby enabling:

- the project plan to be updated with the expenses recorded against each task;
- the cost of each staff member to be calculated and monitored throughout the project;
- the project manager to identify the actual versus budgeted expenditure throughout the project.

On a regular basis, the project administrator updates the project plan with the total expenditure against each task, as listed within the expense register. This enables the project administrator to produce a view of the overall cost of the project to date, and identify any exceptions (such as instances where the actual expenditure exceeds the planned expenditure).

The project administrator then provides the project manager with a copy of the updated project plan and identifies any expenditure deviations noted to date. It is then up to the project manager to take action, based on the extent of the deviation from plan. Examples of actions taken are:

- changing the individual / amount of resource allocated to the task;
- allocating additional funds to complete the task;
- requesting assistance from an external supplier to complete the task;
- raising a project issue for action by the project board / sponsor.

Once each task is completed, it is marked as 100 per cent complete in the project plan and no further expenditure may be allocated to the task for the duration of the project.

Cost management roles

The following roles and responsibilities are involved with the management of costs/ expenses within the project.

Project staff member

Project staff members are responsible for:

- undertaking each delegated task to the best of their ability;
- completing regular expense forms to the level of detail required;
- submitting expense forms to the project manager for approval;

- providing the project manager with further information surrounding the expense if requested.

Project administrator

The project administrator oversees the cost management process by:

- providing all staff with the expense form template for completion;
- ensuring project staff members complete expense forms on time;
- completing expense forms for supplier invoices received;
- forwarding all expense forms to the project manager for approval;
- maintaining the expense register to ensure that all project expenditure information is accurate and up to date;
- entering summarized expense information into the project plan and identifying any exceptions for the project manager's attention;
- arranging payment of each expense once approved.

Project manager

The project manager has overall responsibility for the cost management process, including:

- ensuring that all staff are informed of the cost management process, that they understand when expense forms need to be submitted, to whom and to what level of detail;
- reviewing and approving all expense forms;
- resolving all expense issues with staff members or suppliers and raising any critical expense-related issues with the project sponsor for action.

Cost management documents

Table 4.3 shows a sample expenses form.
   Table 4.4 shows a sample expense register.

4.6 PERFORM QUALITY MANAGEMENT

Quality management process

A quality management process is a method by which the quality of the deliverables and management processes are assured and controlled during a project. The process involves undertaking a variety of reviews to assess and improve the level of quality of project deliverables and processes. More specifically, the quality management process involves:

Table 4.3 Sample expense form

PROJECT DETAILS							
Project name:		*Name of the project incurring this expense*					
Project manager:		*Name of the project manager responsible for this expense*					
Staff member:		*Name of the person submitting this expense form*					
EXPENSE DETAILS							
Activity ID	Task ID	Expense date	Expense type	Expense description	Expense amount	Payee name	Invoice no.
				Total			
APPROVAL DETAILS							

Submitted by   **Approved by**
Name: Name:
Signature: Date: Signature: Date:

_____ __/__/__   _____ __/__/__

Any invoices relating to this expense form should be attached to this document

PLEASE FORWARD THIS FORM TO THE PROJECT MANAGER

Table 4.4 Sample expense register

EXPENSE REGISTER
Project name:
Project manager:

Activity				Expense				Approval				Payment			
Activity ID	Activity description	Task ID	Task description	Expense ID	Expense type	Expense description		Approval status	Approval date	Approver	Payment status	Payment date	Payee	Method		

- listing the quality targets to be achieved from the quality plan;
- identifying the types of quality measurement techniques to be undertaken;
- implementing quality assurance and quality control techniques;
- taking action to enhance the level of deliverable and process quality;
- reporting the level of quality attained.

The quality management process is undertaken during the execution phase of the project. Although quality assurance methods may be initiated prior to this phase, quality control techniques are implemented during the actual construction of each physical deliverable. Without a formal quality management process in place, the basic premise of delivering the project to meet 'time, cost and quality' targets may be compromised. The quality management process is terminated only when all of the deliverables and management processes have been completed.

Figure 4.4 describes the processes and procedures to be undertaken to assure and control the quality of deliverables and processes within the project. Where applicable, quality roles have also been allocated.

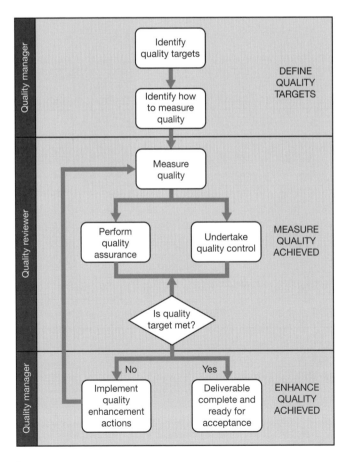

Figure 4.4 Quality management process

Define quality targets

Before undertaking quality management, you should first revisit the quality targets and methods of assuring and controlling quality. Table 4.5 will have already been documented within the quality plan.

Table 4.5 Quality targets

		Quality targets	
Project requirement	**Project deliverable**	**Quality criteria**	**Quality standards**
New financial management solution with accounts receivable and payables processes	Implementation of Oracle Financials General Ledger (GL), Accounts Payable (AP) and Accounts Receivable (AR) system modules	*System functionality:* ● GL tested & installed. ● AP tested & installed. ● AR tested & installed. *System performance:* ● System up-time. ● System response time. ● Data migrated from old system.	*System functionality:* ● GL operational with no errors. ● AP operational with no errors. ● AR operational with no errors. *System performance:* ● 99.9% system uptime. ● < 5 second response times. ● 100% data accuracy.
...	...	...	...

Measure quality achieved

With a clear understanding of the quality targets to be achieved, it is time to execute quality assurance and quality control techniques to assure and control the level of quality of each deliverable constructed.

Perform quality assurance

Use quality assurance (QA) methods to assure the level of quality of project deliverables and processes. QA is defined as 'the *preventive* steps taken to eliminate any variances in the quality of deliverables produced from the quality targets set'. QA techniques are often undertaken at a summarized level of the project by an external project resource. Examples of QA methods are:

- referencing historical data to understand areas where quality issues are likely to occur;
- informing the team of the quality targets defined, to ensure that expectations are set;
- recruiting skilled staff to improve the likelihood of producing high-quality deliverables;
- using change control procedures to minimize the number of potential quality issues;
- undertaking quality reviews to provide confidence that the project is on track.

Undertake quality control

Use quality control (QC) techniques to control the actual level of quality of project deliverables and processes. QC is defined as 'the *curative* steps taken to eliminate any variances in the quality of deliverables produced from the quality targets set'. QC techniques are often undertaken at a detailed level of a project by an internal project resource. Examples of QC methods are undertaking:

- peer reviews;
- deliverable reviews;
- documentation reviews;
- phase reviews;
- process reviews.

Enhance quality achieved

Assess the results of the quality assurance and quality control activities undertaken to determine the actual quality achieved. Compare the level of quality achieved to the targets set, and identify any deviations. If the level of quality achieved does not meet the targets set, then identify and implement a set of quality improvement actions and begin the measurement of quality again. Continue this process until the quality of each deliverable and process meets the quality targets defined. Regardless of the outcome, it is necessary to report the level of quality attained to the project manager for consideration. The project manager will need to be aware of the current level of quality of each deliverable, and record the quality improvement actions in the project plan.

Quality management roles

The following roles and responsibilities are involved with assuring and controlling the level of quality within a project.

Quality manager

The quality manager ensures that the project produces a set of deliverables which attain a specified level of quality as agreed with the customer. The quality manager is responsible for:

- ensuring that comprehensive quality targets are defined for each deliverable;
- implementing QA methods to assure the quality of deliverables to be produced by the project;
- implementing QC techniques to control the quality of the deliverables currently being produced by the project;
- recording the level of quality achieved in the quality register;
- identifying quality deviations and improvement actions for implementation;
- reporting the quality status to the project manager.

Quality reviewer

The quality reviewer identifies the actual level of quality associated with the deliverables produced and notifies the quality manager of any variations from the quality targets set. A quality reviewer may be internal to the project (implementing QC) or external to the project (implementing QA). The quality reviewer is responsible for:

- reviewing the quality of deliverables produced and management processes undertaken;
- informing the quality manager of the level of quality attained for each project deliverable;
- escalating any quality issues identified to the quality manager.

Quality management documents

Quality review forms

Quality reviews are undertaken to provide the customer with confidence that the quality of the deliverables and management processes are acceptable. Quality review forms are used during the quality review process to provide structure around the items being reviewed. The two generic types of quality review forms used within projects are deliverable review forms and process review forms.

Deliverable review form

This form is used to assess the level of quality of the deliverables being created for the client. Deliverable reviews are undertaken at key milestones throughout the project. To achieve the best results, undertake deliverable reviews during the creation of each set of deliverables, as well as at the end of the deliverable construction phase. This will enable quality deviations to be identified earlier, and therefore increase the likelihood of the project achieving the required level of quality within the given timeframes. Document the outcome of each review using Table 4.6.

Process review form

This form is used to assess the level of quality of the management processes undertaken during the course of the project. Process reviews are undertaken at key milestones throughout the project to determine the level of conformance of the actual processes undertaken to the required processes set out in the quality plan. Any deviations are identified and a set of improvement actions are formulated. The outcome of each review is documented using Table 4.7.

Deliverables register

The quality register is the log which records the progress of all deliverables physically constructed. An example is shown as Table 4.8.

4.7 PERFORM CHANGE MANAGEMENT

Change management process

A change management process is a method by which changes to the project scope, deliverables, timescales or resources are identified, evaluated and approved prior to implementation. The process entails completing a variety of control procedures to ensure that if implemented, the change will cause minimal impact to the project.

This process is undertaken during the execution phase of the project, once the project has been formally defined and planned. In theory, any change to the project during the execution phase will need to be formally managed as part of the change process. Without a formal change process in place, the ability of the project manager to effectively manage the scope of the project may be compromised. The change management process is terminated only when the execution phase of the project is complete.

Figure 4.5 shows the processes and procedures to be undertaken to initiate, implement and review changes within the project. Where applicable, change roles have also been identified.

Submit change request

To initiate a change process, you should first allow any member of the project team to submit a request for a change to the project. The person raising the change is called the

Table 4.6 Deliverable review form

Quality target				Quality achieved				
Project requirement	Project deliverable	Quality criteria	Quality standards	Quality level L	M	H	Quality deviation	Improvement recommendation
New financial management solution with accounts receivable and payable processes	Implementation of Oracle Financials General Ledger (GL), Accounts Payable (AP) and Accounts Receivable (AR) system modules	*System functionality* GL tested / installed AP tested / installed AR tested / installed	*System functionality* GL operational, no errors AP operational, no errors AR operational, no errors	x	x	x	Critical errors currently experienced Implementation part-complete only No deviation.	Reinstall GL system to remove critical errors Complete system implementation No further action required
		System performance System up-time System response time Data accuracy	*System performance* 99.9% system up-time <1 second response time 100% data accuracy	x	x	x	System up-time only 90% 5 second response times No deviation. Data 100% accurate	New hardware required to increase stability New hardware required to improve response times No further action required
…	…	…	…	…	…	…	…	…

Table 4.7 Process review form

Quality target				Quality achieved				
Project process	Project procedure	Quality criteria	Quality standards	Quality level L	M	H	Quality deviation	Improvement recommendation
Risk management	Risk procedures: • Identify risk.	• % of 'medium' and 'high' level risks identified.	• 100% of 'medium' and 'high' level risks identified.	☐	☐	☐	• Only 75% of 'medium' and 'high' level risks identified.	• Hold weekly risk review meetings to ensure that all 'medium' and 'high' level risks are identified.
	• Submit risk form.	• % of risk forms completed for risks identified.	• 100% of risk forms completed for risks identified.	☐	☐	☐	• No deviation. A risk form was completed for every risk identified.	• No further action required.
	• Review risk.	• % of risks formally tracked via risk register.	• 100% of risks formally tracked via risk register.	☐	☐	☐	• No deviation. All risks identified were tracked in the risk register.	• No further action required.
	• Confirm risk is applicable to project.	• % of risks adequately mitigated.	• 90% of risks adequately mitigated prior to the risk happening.	☐	☐	☐	• Only 50% of risks identified were reduced through risk mitigating actions.	• At each risk review meeting, allocate (and track) actions which mitigate each risk identified.
...	...	...	...	☐	☐	☐	...	...

Table 4.8 Quality register

QUALITY REGISTER
Project name:
Project manager:
Quality manager:

ID	Summary		Quality targets		Quality assurance			Quality control		
	Deliverable name	Deliverable description	Status	Criteria	Standards	Reviewer	Review date	Review outcome	Reviewer	Review date	Review outcome

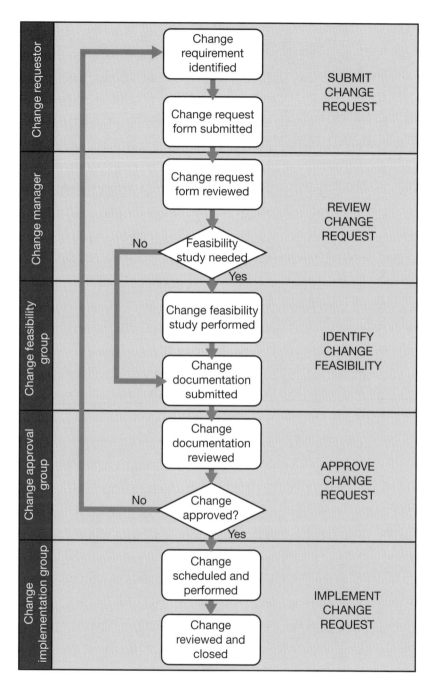

Figure 4.5 Change management process

'change requester'. The change requester will document the requirement for change to the project by completing a change request form (CRF), summarizing the change description, benefits, costs, impact and approvals required.

Review change request

The change manager reviews the CRF and determines whether or not a feasibility study is required for the change approval group to assess the full impact of the change. The decision will be based on the size and complexity of the change proposed. The change manager will record the CRF details in the change register.

Identify change feasibility

If deemed necessary, a change feasibility study is completed to determine the extent to which the change requested is actually feasible. The change feasibility study will define in detail the change requirements, options, costs, benefits, risks, issues, impact, recommendations and plan. All change documentation is then collated by the change manager and submitted to the change approval group for final review. This includes the original CRF, the approved change feasibility study report and any supporting documentation.

Approve change request

A formal review of the CRF is undertaken by the change approval group. The change approval group will either reject the change, request more information related to the change, approve the change as requested or approve the change subject to specified conditions. Their decision will be based on the level of risk and impact to the project resulting from both implementing and not implementing the change.

Implement change request

Approved changes are then implemented. This involves:

- identifying a date for implementation of the change;
- implementing the change;
- reviewing and communicating the success of the change implementation;
- recording all change actions in the change register.

Change roles

The following roles and responsibilities are involved with the management of change within the project.

Change requester

The change requester initially recognizes a need for change to the project and formally communicates this requirement to the change manager. The change requester is responsible for:

- identifying the need to make a change to the project;
- documenting the need for change by completing a CRF;
- submitting the CRF to the change manager for review.

Change manager

The change manager receives, logs, monitors and controls the progress of all changes within a project. The change manager is responsible for:

- receiving all CRFs and logging them in the change register;
- categorizing and prioritizing all change requests;
- reviewing all CRFs to determine whether additional information is required;
- determining whether or not a formal change feasibility study is required;
- forwarding the CRF to the change approval group for approval;
- escalating all CRF issues and risks to the change approval group;
- reporting and communicating all decisions made by the change approval group.

Change feasibility group

The change feasibility group complete feasibility studies for CRFs issued by the change manager. The change feasibility group is responsible for:

- undertaking research to determine the likely options for change, costs, benefits and impacts of the change;
- documenting all findings within a feasibility study report;
- forwarding the feasibility study report to the change manager for change approval group submission.

Change approval group

The change approval group is the principal authority for all CRFs forwarded by the change manager. The change approval group is responsible for:

- reviewing all CRFs forwarded by the change manager;
- considering all supporting documentation;
- approving or rejecting each CRF based on its relevant merits;
- resolving change conflict, where two or more changes overlap;
- identifying the implementation timetable for approved changes.

Change implementation group

The change implementation group will schedule and implement all changes. The change implementation group is responsible for:

- scheduling all changes within the timeframes provided by the change approval group;
- testing all changes, prior to implementation;
- implementing all changes within the project;
- reviewing the success of each change, following implementation;
- requesting that the change manager close the change in the change register.

Change documents

Change request form

A CRF is completed by a member of a project to request a change to the project. An example is provided as Figure 4.6.

Change register

A change register is a log where all requests for change are registered and tracked through to implementation. An example is provided as Table 4.9.

4.8 PERFORM RISK MANAGEMENT

Risk management process

A risk management process is a method by which risks to the project are formally identified, quantified and managed during the execution of the project. The process entails completing a number of actions to reduce the likelihood of occurrence and the severity of impact of each risk. A risk process is used to ensure that every risk is formally identified, quantified, monitored, avoided, transferred and/or mitigated.

Although a risk process is undertaken during the execution phase of the project, risks may be identified at any stage of the project life cycle. In theory, any risk identified during the life of the project will need to be formally managed as part of the risk management process. Without a risk management process in place, unforeseen risks may impact the ability of the project to meet its objectives. The risk management process is terminated only when the execution phase of the project is completed.

Figure 4.7 provides an overview of the risk processes and procedures to be undertaken to effectively manage project-related risks. Risk roles have also been identified.

PROJECT DETAILS		
Project name:	*Name of the project against which the change is being requested*	
Project manager:	*Name of the project manager responsible for implementing the change*	

CHANGE DETAILS

Change no:	*Unique identifier for the change (as per change register)*
Change requester:	*Name of person who is requesting the change*
Change request date:	*Date on which this form is completed*
Change urgency:	*Urgency for undertaking the change*

Change description:	Change drivers:
Brief description of the change requested	*List any drivers which necessitate this change*
Change benefits:	Change costs:
Describe the benefits associated with the change	*Describe the costs associated with the change*

IMPACT DETAILS

Project impact:
Describe the impact on the project if this change is / not implemented

APPROVAL DETAILS

Supporting documentation:
Reference any supporting documentation used to substantiate this change

Submitted by		**Approved by**	
Name:		Name:	
Signature:	Date:	Signature:	Date:
_____	__ / / __	_____	__ / / __

PLEASE FORWARD THIS FORM TO THE CHANGE MANAGER

Figure 4.6   Change request form

Table 4.9 Change register

CHANGE REGISTER
Project name:
Project manager:
Change manager:

Summary			Description				Approval				Implementation		
ID	Date raised	Raised by	Received by	Description of change	Description of impact	Impact rating	Change approver(s)	Approval status	Approval date	Implementation resource	Implementation status	Implementation date

Raise risk

To initiate a risk management process, you should first allow any member of the project team to raise a project-related risk. The person raising the risk is called the 'risk origina- tor'. The risk originator identifies a risk applicable to a particular aspect of the project (its scope, deliverables, timescales or resources) and completes a risk form describing the nature of the risk identified.

Register risk

The project manager reviews all risks raised and determines whether or not each risk identified is applicable to the project. This decision will be primarily based upon whether or not the risk impacts on the:

- deliverable specified in the quality register;
- quality targets specified in the quality plan;
- timeframes specified in the project plan;
- resource targets specified in the resource plan;
- financial targets specified in the financial plan.

If the risk is considered by the project manager to be valid, then the risk is documented in the risk register and a risk Id is assigned. The project manager will assign a level of 'impact' and 'likelihood' to the risk, based upon the predicted risk severity.

Assign risk actions

The project review group then complete a formal review of each risk listed in the risk register and decide based on the risk impact and likelihood, whether to:

- assign risk actions to mitigate the risk;
- raise a change request if a change to the project is required to mitigate the risk;
- close the risk in the risk register, if there are no outstanding risk actions and the risk is no longer likely to impact on the project.

Implement risk actions

All risk mitigating actions assigned by the project review group are then implemented. This involves:

- scheduling each action for implementation;
- implementing each action scheduled;
- reviewing the success of each action implemented;

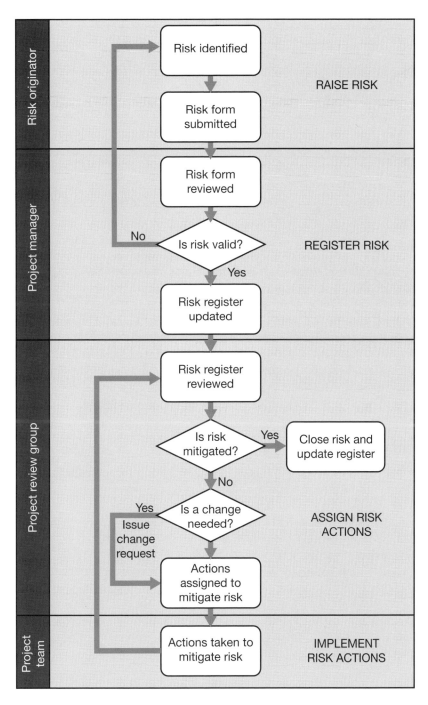

Figure 4.7 Risk management process

- communicating the success of each action implemented.

Risk roles

The following roles and responsibilities are involved with the management of risk within the project.

Risk originator

The risk originator identifies a project risk, documents the risk by completing a risk form and submits the risk form to the project manager for review.

Project manager

The project manager receives each risk form and monitors the progress of all risks within the project. The project manager is responsible for:

- receiving all risk forms and identifying whether the risk is appropriate to the project;
- recording all risks in the risk register and monitoring the status of the risk thereafter;
- presenting all risks to the project review group;
- communicating all decisions made by the project review group;
- monitoring the progress of all risk mitigating actions assigned.

Project review group

The project review group assess the risk likelihood and impact ratings and then assign risk mitigating actions where appropriate. The project review group is responsible for:

- the regular review of all risks recorded in the risk register;
- identifying change requests required to mitigate risks raised;
- allocating risk mitigating actions;
- closing risks which are no longer likely to impact on the project.

Project team

The project team undertake all risk mitigating actions delegated by the project review group.

Risk documents

Risk form

A risk form is completed by a member of a project to raise a new project risk. An example is provided as Figure 4.8.

Risk register

The risk register is the log within which all risks are registered and tracked through to closure. An example is provided as Table 4.10.

4.9 PERFORM ISSUE MANAGEMENT

Issue management process

An issue management process is a method by which issues that are currently affecting the ability of the project to produce the required deliverables are formally managed. The process entails completing a variety of review methods to assess the level of impact that the issue is having on the project. A number of actions are then taken to resolve or reduce the issue as appropriate. The issue process is used to ensure that every issue identified is formally communicated, documented, monitored, reviewed and resolved.

Although the issue process is undertaken during the execution phase of the project, issues may be identified at any stage of the project life cycle. In theory, any issue identified during the life of the project will need to be managed under the issue management process. Without an issue process in place, unforeseen issues may negatively affect the ability of the project to achieve the stated objectives.

The issue management process is terminated only when the execution phase is complete. Figure 4.9 describes the processes and procedures to be undertaken to identify, document, prioritize and resolve issues within the project. Where applicable, issue roles have also been identified.

Raise issue

To initiate an issue process, you should first allow any member of the team to raise a project-related issue. The person raising the issue is called the 'issue originator'. The issue originator identifies an issue applicable to a particular aspect of the project and completes an issue form to be sent to the project manager.

PROJECT DETAILS

Project name: *Name of the project against which the risk relates*
Project manager: *Name of the project manager responsible for mitigating the risk*

RISK DETAILS

Risk ID: *Unique identifier assigned to this risk*
Raised by: *Name of person who is raising the risk*
Date raised: *Date this form is completed*

Risk description:
Add a brief description of the risk identified and its likely impact on the project scope, resources, deliverables, timescales and/or budgets.

Risk likelihood: Risk impact:
Describe and rate the likelihood of the risk   *Describe and rate the impact on the project if*
eventuating   *the risk eventuates*

RISK MITIGATION

Recommended preventive actions:
Add a brief description of the actions to be taken to prevent the risk from eventuating

Recommended contingent actions:
Add a brief description of the actions to be taken should the risk eventuate, to minimize the impact on the project

APPROVAL DETAILS

Supporting documentation:
Reference any supporting documentation used to substantiate this risk

Signature: **Date:**

_____   ___/___/___

PLEASE FORWARD THIS FORM TO THE PROJECT MANAGER

Figure 4.8   Risk form

Table 4.10 Risk register

RISK REGISTER
Project name:
Project manager:

	Summary			Description					Prevention action				Contingency actions			
ID	Date raised	Raised by	Received by	Description of Risk	Description of impact	Likelihood rating	Impact rating	Priority rating	Preventive actions	Action resource	Action date	Contingency actions	Action resource	Action date		

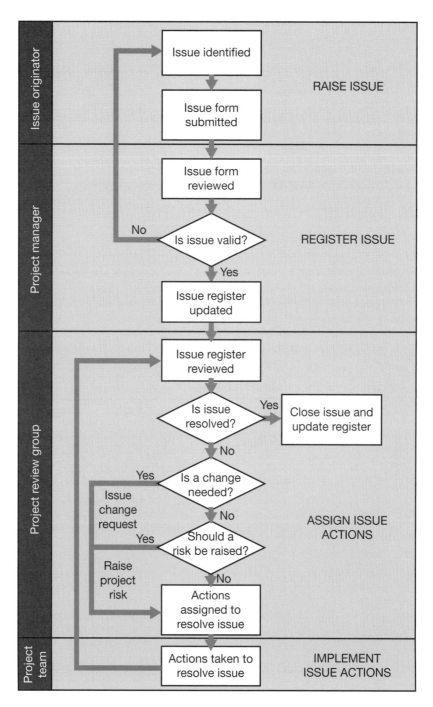

Figure 4.9 Issue management process

Register issue

The project manager reviews all issues raised and determines whether or not each issue is applicable to the project. This decision is based on whether or not the issue impacts on:

- a deliverable specified in the quality register;
- the quality targets specified in the quality plan;
- the timeframes specified in the project plan;
- the resource targets specified in the resource plan;
- the financial targets specified in the financial plan.

If the issue is considered by the project manager to be valid, then the issue is documented in the issue register and an issue number assigned. The project manager will assign an issue priority based upon the level of impact of the issue to the project.

Assign issue actions

The project review group formally reviews each issue listed in the issue register based on the issue priority, and may decide:

- to assign issue actions to attempt to resolve the issue;
- to raise a change request if the issue results in the need for a change to the project;
- to raise a project risk if the issue is likely to impact on the project in the future;
- to close the issue in the issue register if there are no outstanding actions and the issue is no longer impacting on the project.

Implement issue actions

The actions assigned by the project review group are then implemented. This entails:

- scheduling each action for completion;
- implementing each action scheduled;
- reviewing the success of each action completed;
- communicating the success of each action completed.

Issue roles

The following roles and responsibilities are involved with the management of issues within the project.

Issue originator

The issue originator identifies a project issue, documents the issue by completing an issue form and submits the issue form to the project manager for review.

Project manager

The project manager receives each issue form and monitors the progress of all issues within the project. The project manager is responsible for:

- receiving all issue forms and identifying whether the issue is appropriate to the project;
- recording all issues in the issue register and monitoring its status thereafter;
- presenting all issues to the project review group;
- communicating all decisions made by the project review group;
- monitoring the progress of all actions assigned.

Project review group

The project review group assesses each issue raised and approves a set of actions to resolve them. The project review group is responsible for:

- regularly reviewing all issues recorded in the issue register;
- identifying issues which require change requests and / or project risks to be raised;
- approving issue resolution actions;
- closing issues which no longer impact on the project.

Project team

The project team undertake all issue resolution actions delegated by the project review group.

Issue documents

Issue form

An issue form is completed by a member of a project to raise with management a new project issue. An example is provided as Figure 4.10.

Issue register

The issue register is the log where all issues are registered and tracked through to resolution. An example is provided as Table 4.11.

PROJECT DETAILS

Project name: *Name of the project to which the issue relates*
Project manager: *Name of the project manager responsible for resolving the issue*

ISSUE DETAILS

Issue ID: *Unique identifier for this issue*
Raised by: *Name of person who is raising the issue*
Date raised: *Date on which this form is completed*

Issue description:
Add a brief description of the issue identified and the aspect of the project currently impacted (e.g. scope, resources, deliverables, timescales and/or budgets).

Issue impact:
Describe the effect that the issue is having on the project's ability to meet its stated objectives. Rate the level of impact of the issue (i.e. low, medium or high) on the project

ISSUE RESOLUTION

Recommended actions:
Add a brief description of all actions required to resolve the issue identified.

APPROVAL DETAILS

Supporting documentation:
Reference any supporting documentation used to substantiate this issue

Signature: **Date:**

_____   ____/ /____

PLEASE FORWARD THIS FORM TO THE PROJECT MANAGER

Figure 4.10   Issue form

Table 4.11 Issue register

ISSUE REGISTER
Project name:
Project manager:

	Summary			Description			Resolution				
ID	Date raised	Raised by	Status	Description of issue	Impact	Priority	Action	Owner	Outcome	Date for resolution	Date resolved

4.10 PERFORM PROCUREMENT MANAGEMENT

Procurement management process

The procurement management process is the method by which products are acquired for a project from external suppliers. The process involves controlling the ordering, receipt, review and approval of products from suppliers as well as managing the overall performance of the supplier.

A procurement process is used to ensure that all products are acquired within the correct timescales, to the level of quality defined and within the budgeted cost identified. The process also sets out the procedures for ensuring that supplier relationships are properly managed, through the regular review of supplier performance and resolution of supplier issues.

The procurement process is initiated after the procurement plan has been approved and the supplier contract signed. The procurement process is usually managed by a single resource within the project (such as a procurement officer or manager) and overseen by the project manager.

Without a formal procurement process in place, it will be difficult to confirm that the products provided by the supplier are 'fit for purpose' and therefore meet the requirements outlined within the procurement plan. It will also be difficult to identify and manage supplier issues, and this will therefore increase the overall level of risk to the project. The procurement process is terminated only when the execution phase is complete.

Figure 4.11 describes the processes and procedures required to manage the procurement of products from suppliers for the project. Where applicable, procurement roles have also been identified. Note that this process caters for the procurement of all types of products, including 'goods' (such as computer hardware, raw materials and equipment) and 'services' (such as raw labour, technical services, consultancy and management).

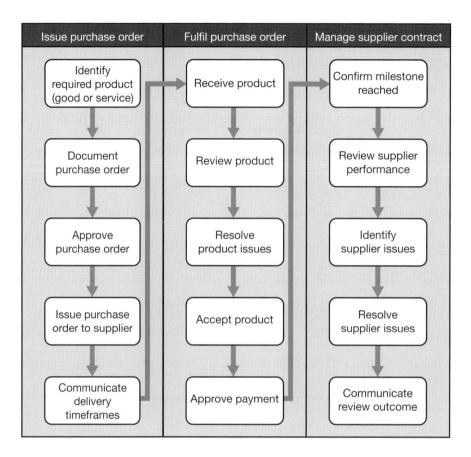

Figure 4.11 Procurement management process

Issue purchase order

The first process initiated to purchase product from a supplier is the creation and issue of a purchase order.

Identify required product

The procurement manager identifies the products to be purchased and their suppliers from the procurement plan. He or she also identifies the timeframes within which the products must be delivered and the level of quality that each product should adhere to.

Document purchase order

To request product from an external supplier, the procurement manager must complete a purchase order form. This form lists the specific product required, the components, delivery timeframes, delivery address and project cost centre to be charged for its purchase. A purchase order form may be completed for several products, but each form is used for only one supplier. It is important that the purchase order is completed well before the required delivery date to give the supplier the maximum notice period possible and therefore increase the likelihood of the delivery occurring on time.

Approve purchase order

The purchase order is then forwarded to the project manager for approval. The project manager will consider the following criteria prior to approving the form:

- Is the product listed as a required product in the procurement plan?
- Is the product defined in sufficient detail for the supplier to interpret the requirement?
- Is there likely to be sufficient time for the supplier to deliver the product and meet the timeframes outlined in the procurement plan?
- Does the project have a contractual relationship with the supplier?

Issue purchase order to supplier

Once the purchase order is approved by the project manager, it is issued to the supplier for fulfilment.

Communicate delivery timeframes

The supplier then confirms receipt of the purchase order and issues an ETA (estimated time of arrival) for the product(s). The ETA describes the likely timeframe for delivery of the product to the designated project location.

Fulfil purchase order

The purchase order is then processed by the supplier and the product is delivered to the project as ordered. The procurement manager reviews the product and identifies and resolves any product issues. The product is then accepted and supplier payment is authorized.

Receive product

The supplier fulfils the order by delivering the product as defined by the purchase order to the project. The procurement manager physically views the product received and confirms that the project team have received it into their care. In the case of a service delivered by the supplier, the procurement manager confirms from the project team that the service has been performed and is ready for review.

Review product

The product is then reviewed to determine whether or not it meets the requirements of the purchase order. This may involve a physical inspection (in the case of a good) or a series of interviews (in the case of a service) to determine that the product was delivered on time, within cost and at the level of quality required.

Resolve product issues

If the outcome of the review is that one or many of the requirements set out by the purchase order have not been satisfactorily achieved, then an issue is raised by the procurement manager. The extent of the problem is then quantified and the impact and severity of the issue is rated. The project manager will then lead the resolution of the issue to ensure that it is quickly and appropriately resolved.

Accept product

Once all product delivery issues have been resolved, the project manager will accept the product on behalf of the project team and notify the supplier.

Approve payment

The supplier will then send the project team an invoice, which is approved for payment by the project manager.

Manage supplier contract

The above procedures are undertaken for each purchase order issued by the project. In parallel to the purchase order process, the overall performance of the supplier is assessed to determine whether it is continuing to meet its commitments outlined in the contract.

Confirm milestone reached

A number of supplier review milestones will have already been identified and documented as part of the procurement plan. Review milestones may be triggered by the completion of a particular project phase, deliverable or date. Once each milestone is reached, the procurement manager informs the project manager that the supplier's performance is ready to be assessed, and a formal assessment programme is initiated.

Review supplier performance

The procurement manager reviews the supplier's performance by:

- confirming that the review milestone has in fact been reached;
- identifying the products provided by the supplier and assessing whether or not they met the requirements of the purchase order;
- confirming that each condition listed within the supplier contract has been met.

Identify supplier issues

Any issues identified during the review are listed and the impact on the project is quantified. The issues are then documented and formally raised with the project manager for resolution.

Resolve supplier issues

The project manager then oversees the resolution of each issue by helping the procurement manager to negotiate a resolution with the supplier. There could be any of the following outcomes:

- The supplier is congratulated on its performance if no supplier issues were identified.
- The supplier is informed that should further issues occur, payment will be withheld and the contract may be terminated.
- Supplier payment is withheld and a dispute is initiated under the terms of the contract. Legal action may also be commenced by either the project manager or the supplier.

Communicate review outcome

Once the review is complete and any issues resolved, the outcome of the review is communicated to key project stakeholders.

Procurement roles

The following roles and responsibilities are involved with project procurement.

Procurement manager

The procurement manager is responsible for ensuring that the entire procurement process is undertaken effectively by:

- identifying products to be sourced from external suppliers;
- documenting each purchase order and forwarding it to the project manager for approval;
- issuing the purchase order to the supplier and communicating the delivery timeframes;
- receiving and reviewing the product upon arrival at the designated project location;
- accepting the product and requesting the approval of supplier payment;
- reviewing the supplier performance and identifying any contractual issues for action;
- identifying and resolving product delivery issues.

Project manager

The project manager oversees the procurement process by:

- approving each purchase order as presented by the procurement manager;
- approving each payment as requested by the procurement manager;
- assisting the procurement manager with the resolution of supplier issues.

Procurement documents

Purchase order form

A purchase order form is completed to purchase product from an external supplier. Although one purchase order form can be completed per product, a purchase order form may also be completed for a set of products to be sourced from a single supplier. An example is provided as Figure 4.12.

Procurement register

The procurement register is the log where all purchase orders are registered and tracked through to approval. An example is provided as Table 4.12.

4.11 PERFORM ACCEPTANCE MANAGEMENT

Acceptance management process

An acceptance management process is a method by which deliverables produced by the project are reviewed and accepted by the customer. The process entails completing a variety of review techniques to confirm that the deliverable meets the acceptance criteria outlined in the acceptance plan. An acceptance process is used to ensure that every deliverable produced by the project is 100 per cent complete and has been reviewed and approved by the customer.

The acceptance process is undertaken towards the end of the execution phase of the project, as each deliverable is presented to the customer for final sign-off. Depending on the project, one of several approaches may be taken for deliverable acceptance:

- Each deliverable may be reviewed and presented individually to the customer for sign-off.
- Sets of deliverables may be reviewed and presented for acceptance at the same time.
- All project deliverables may be reviewed and presented for acceptance at the same time.

Without a formal acceptance process in place, the customer may not accept the final deliverables produced by the project, thereby compromising the project's overall success. The acceptance process is terminated only when the execution phase is complete. Figure 4.13 describes the processes and procedures required to gain the acceptance of project deliverables by the customer. Where applicable, acceptance roles have also been identified.

PURCHASE DETAILS

Purchase order #:
Purchase order date:
Required by date:

DELIVERY DETAILS

From:	To:
Project name:	*Supplier name:*
Project address:	*Supplier address:*
Project contact name:	*Supplier contact name:*
Project contact ph. no.:	*Supplier contact ph. no.:*

Deliver to:	Bill to:
Delivery contact name:	*Billing contact name:*
Delivery address:	*Billing address:*

ORDER DETAILS

Item	Description	Quantity	Unit price	Total price
			Subtotal:	
			Other:	
			Total:	

PAYMENT DETAILS

Payment method: *Method of payment offered (eg credit card, cheque, direct debit, cash)*

Credit card details:
Card type: (*Visa/MasterCard/Amex/Other*)
Card number: xxxx-xxxx-xxxx-xxxx
Expiry date: xx/xx
Name on card: xxxxxxxxxxxxxxxxxxxxx

TERMS AND CONDITIONS

List any terms and conditions applicable to this purchase order. For example:

● To validate this purchase order, the supplier must confirm the purchase of each item listed above and the estimated delivery timescales within 24 hours of receipt of this order and prior to the delivery of the product.
● This purchase order must be completed to the satisfaction of the receiver before payment is due.
● (Reference the supplier contract against which this purchase order has been raised).

Figure 4.12   Purchase order form

Table 4.12 Procurement register

PROCUREMENT REGISTER
Project name:
Project manager:
Procurement manager:

	Product						Supplier			Order					Payment		
PO #	Item title	Item description	Quantity	Unit price	Total price	Required by date	Company	Contact name	Contact ph. no.	PO status	PO date	Delivery status	Delivery date	Payment methods	Payment status	Payment date	

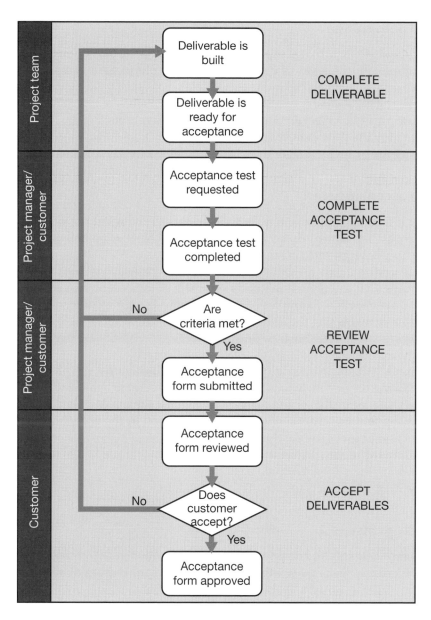

Figure 4.13 Acceptance management process

Complete deliverable

Before you request the formal acceptance of a deliverable by a customer, the deliverable must be completed to a level of quality which is likely to gain customer acceptance. This involves:

- undertaking all tasks required to complete the deliverable;
- documenting the final deliverable components;
- informing the project manager that the deliverable is ready for customer acceptance.

Complete acceptance test

The project manager arranges an acceptance test (or review) of the deliverable by the customer to gain agreement that the deliverable matches the acceptance criteria and is now ready for final sign-off. This involves:

- Confirming that the review methods outlined in the acceptance plan are still relevant and appropriate. Examples of review methods may include:
  - Physically inspecting the *deliverable.*
  - Auditing the deliverable by a third party.
  - Analysing the *processes* used to create the deliverable.
  - Reviewing the *time* taken to create the deliverable against the project plan.
  - Reviewing the *cost* incurred in creating the deliverable against the financial plan.
  - Reviewing the *quality* of the deliverable against the quality plan.
- Confirming that the criteria and resources outlined in the acceptance plan are still relevant and appropriate for the review.
- Scheduling the review with the customer.
- Undertaking the review with the customer.
- Documenting the results to present to the customer.

Review acceptance test

The acceptance test results are assessed by the customer to determine whether or not they met the criteria specified within the acceptance plan. This involves:

- comparing the results against the original acceptance criteria;
- determining whether or not those criteria have been met;
- initiating further work required to improve the deliverable if required;
- completing an acceptance form for deliverable approval.

Accept deliverable

The deliverable is then finally accepted by the customer. This involves:

- reviewing the acceptance form to ensure that all final criteria have been met;
- obtaining acceptance form approval from the customer;
- transferring the deliverable to the customer environment.

Acceptance roles

The following roles and responsibilities are involved with gaining customer acceptance for deliverables within the project.

Project manager

The project manager oversees the entire acceptance process for all deliverables produced by the project. The project manager is responsible for:

- receiving notification from the project team that the deliverable is complete and ready for customer acceptance;
- organizing the acceptance review of the deliverable with the customer, scheduling the resources and documenting the results;
- completing the acceptance form for customer sign-off;
- managing the tasks required to transfer the deliverable from the project to the customer environment.

Customer

The customer is the final approval authority. The customer is responsible for:

- undertaking the acceptance review (where possible);
- authorizing the acceptance form to provide final confirmation that the deliverable has met the criteria specified within the acceptance plan;
- taking custody of the deliverable within the business environment.

Acceptance documents

To help you undertake acceptance management, a sample acceptance form and acceptance register are provided.

Acceptance form

An acceptance form is completed to request formal acceptance of a project deliverable by the customer. An example is provided as Figure 4.14.

Acceptance register

The acceptance register is the log within which all acceptance requests are registered and tracked through to approval. An example is provided as Table 4.13.

PROJECT DETAILS

Project name: *Name of project which produced the deliverable.*
Project manager: *Name of the project manager responsible for producing the deliverable.*

ACCEPTANCE DETAILS

Acceptance ID: *Unique identifier for this acceptance request*
Requested by: *Name of person who is requesting deliverable acceptance*
Date requested: *Date within which this form is submitted for approval*

Description:
Add a brief description of the deliverable for which customer acceptance is being requested.

ACCEPTANCE CRITERIA

Criteria: Standards:
List the criteria against which the   *List the standards against which the*
deliverable has been measured.   *deliverable has been measured.*

ACCEPTANCE RESULTS

For each criteria and standard identified above, list the:
- *methods used to assess whether or not the deliverable meets such criteria and standards;*
- *reviewer who was formally responsible for undertaking the acceptance review;*
- *date on which the review was completed and the overall result (failed, passed or exceeded expectations).*

Acceptance	Method	Reviewer	Date	Result
Criteria • •				
Standard • •				

Supporting documentation:
Reference any supporting documentation used to substantiate this acceptance request.

Signature: **Date:**

_____   __/__/__

PLEASE FORWARD THIS FORM TO THE CUSTOMER FOR APPROVAL

Figure 4.14 Acceptance form

Table 4.13   Acceptance register

ACCEPTANCE REGISTER
Customer:
Project name:
Project manager:
Quality manager:

	Deliverable			Acceptance criteria			Acceptance test			Acceptance results	
ID	Deliverable name	Deliverable description	Status	Criteria	Standards	Method	Reviewer	Date	Results	Status

4.12 PERFORM COMMUNICATIONS MANAGEMENT

Communications management process

A communications management process is a method by which formal messages are identified, created, reviewed and communicated within a project. Clear, accurate and timely communication is critical to the success of any project, as miscommunication can result in increased project risk. Clear project communication therefore ensures that the correct stakeholders have the right information, at the right time, with which to make well-informed decisions.

Various types of formal communication may be undertaken in a project. Examples are releasing regular project status or performance reports, communicating project risks, issues and changes, and summarizing project information in weekly newsletters. Regardless of the type of communication to be undertaken, the method for undertaking the communication will always remain the same:

- Identify the message content, audience, timing and format.
- Create the message to be sent.
- Review the message prior to distribution.
- Communicate the message to the recipients.

These four processes should be applied to any type of formal communication on the project, including the distribution of:

- regular project status reports;
- results of phase review meetings;
- quality review reports documented;
- minutes of all project team meetings;
- newsletters and other general communication items.

Although the communications process is typically undertaken after the communications plan has been documented, communications will take place during all phases of the project. This process therefore applies to all formal communications undertaken during the life of the project. Without a formal communications management process in place, it will be difficult to ensure that project stakeholders receive the right information at the right time.

Figure 4.15 illustrates the processes and procedures to be undertaken to identify, create, review and communicate key messages within the project. Where applicable, communications roles have also been identified.

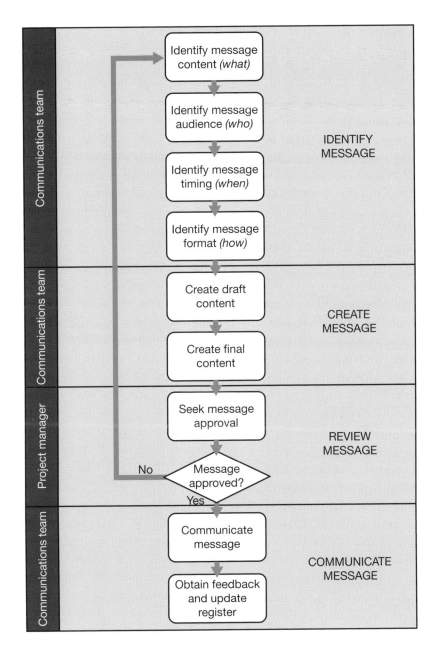

Figure 4.15 Communications management process

Identify message

Communications management begins with the identification of the message content, audience, timing and format for approval and distribution to a particular project stakeholder group.

Identify message content

First, a need for communication is identified. Anyone in the project can identify a communications need. However the project manager must agree that the need is real and a formal message should be distributed to the relevant stakeholders. The specific message content is then documented. Examples of types of message content include:

- activity status or financial status information;
- deliverables or milestones status information;
- supplier performance and procurement status;
- risks, issues and changes identified.

Identify message audience

Next, the target audience are identified. Examples of target audiences include:

- project administration team;
- project review group;
- entire project team;
- all project stakeholders.

Identify message timing

At this point, the type of content to be distributed and the audience have been clearly specified. The next step is to identify the timing or frequency of the communications message. In some cases it may be necessary to have regular communications messages, such as weekly project status reports or monthly newsletters, whereas in other cases a one-off communication event may be satisfactory, such as the notification of a change in project office premises. In each case, the project manager will need to be satisfied that the regularity of the message is suitable, based on the message content and audience.

Identify message format

Finally, the communication format is identified. A number of different types of formats are available including verbal presentations, written reports, letters and e-mails.

Create message

The first draft of the content is created by the communications team. The communications manager reviews the content and forwards changes to the communications team for further enhancements. The final draft of the message is then drawn up by the communications team and submitted by the communications manager to the project manager for approval and release.

Review message

Depending on the project size and type of message to be distributed, the project manager may or may not be empowered to approve the message for distribution. Examples of types of messages that the project manager is typically empowered to communicate include:

- regular project status;
- project risks and issues;
- requests for project changes;
- regular project news items.

Certain types of messages however may require project review group approval prior to distribution, such as:

- changes to the project scope, objectives or timeframes;
- critical project risks or issues identified;
- major project overspending or delays;
- the premature closure of the project.

Communicate message

The message is approved and dispatched to the target audience, using the approved communication method. After dispatch, the communications register is updated to record the communications event. Feedback is received regarding the message sent, to ensure that it achieved the desired results.

Communications roles

The following roles and responsibilities are involved with undertaking project communications.

Communications team

The communications team construct each communications message and make alterations as requested by the communications manager. They are responsible for:

- formally documenting each communications message;
- making alterations to each communications message as required;
- publishing the final approved message;
- distributing the published message to the specified target audience.

Communications manager

The communications manager oversees the communications team by reviewing all communications messages prior to approval. This includes:

- assisting the project manager with identifying the content, audience, timing and format of all required project communications;
- reviewing all communications items and recommending final changes;
- submitting the final draft to the project manager for approval.

Project manager

The project manager has sole responsibility for ensuring the release of accurate and timely communications messages within the project. This includes:

- documenting a communications plan early in the project;
- identifying the content, audience, timing and format of communications;
- approving or obtaining the approval of all communications messages;
- receiving feedback regarding communications messages released.

Communications documents

Project status report

The project status report is used by project managers to formally communicate the status of a project. It provides a single view of the progress of the project, and ensures that all stakeholders are regularly informed of the progress, issues and risks inherent within the project. The report should be generated on a regular basis throughout the execution phase. Only summarized information that is pertinent to the recipients of the report should be included. For larger projects, several reports may be generated for different stakeholder groups, over different reporting periods. For instance, the project manager may report weekly to the project sponsor and monthly to the project steering committee. An example is shown as Figure 4.16.

PROJECT DETAILS	
Project name: Project ID: Project sponsor: Project manager:	Report recipient: Report prepared by: Report preparation date: Report period:

Project description:
Summarize the overall project achievements, risks and issues experienced to date.

OVERALL STATUS

Overall status:	*[Description]*
Project schedule:	*[Description]*
Project expenses:	*[Description]*
Project deliverables:	*[Description]*
Project risks:	*[Description]*
Project issues:	*[Description]*
Project changes:	*[Description]*

DETAILED STATUS

Project schedule

Milestone	Baseline	Actual	Actual variance	Forecast	Forecast variance	Status
Description	*Description*	*Date*	*Days*	*Date*	*Days*	

Project expenses

Type	Baseline	Actual	Actual variance	Forecast	Forecast variance	Status
Operating (OPEX)	$	$	$	$	$	
Capital (CAPEX)	$	$	$	$	$	

Figure 4.16   Project status report

Project staffing

Activity	Baseline	Actual	Actual variance	Forecast	Forecast variance	Status
Description	*Days effort*	*Days effort*	*Days effort*	*Days effort*	*Days effort*	

Project deliverables

Deliverable	Quality target	Quality achieved	Quality variance	% complete	Status
Description	*Description*	*Description*	*Description*		

Project risks

Risk	Likelihood	Impact	Status
Description	*L/M/H*	*L/M/H*	

Project issues

Issue	Impact	Status
Description	*L/M/H*	

Figure 4.16 *continued*

Communications register

The communications register is the log where all communications messages are recorded for the project. An example is provided as Table 4.14.

Table 4.14 Communications register

COMMUNICATIONS REGISTER
Project name:
Project manager:
Communications manager:

	Summary						Description		
ID	Status	Date approved	Approved by	Date sent	Sent by	Sent to	Type	Message	File location	Feedback

4.13 PERFORM A PHASE REVIEW

At the end of the project execution phase, a phase review is performed. This is a check-point to ensure that the project has achieved its stated objectives as planned. A phase review form is completed to request approval to proceed to the next phase of a project. The form should describe the status of the:

- overall project;
- project schedule based on the project plan;
- project expenses based on the financial plan;
- project staffing based on the resource plan;
- project deliverables based on the quality plan;
- project risks based on the risk register;
- project issues based on the issues register.

The review form should be completed by the project manager and approved by the project sponsor. To obtain approval, the project manager will usually present the current status of the project to the project board for consideration. The project board (chaired by the project sponsor) may decide to cancel the project, undertake further work within the existing project phase or grant approval to begin the next phase of the project.

A phase review form for the project execution phase is shown as Figure 4.17.

PROJECT DETAILS	
Project name: Project manager: Project sponsor:	Report prepared by: Report preparation date: Reporting period:

Project description:
[Summarize the overall project achievements, risks and issues experienced to date.]

OVERALL STATUS

Overall status: *[Description]*
Project schedule: *[Description]*
Project expenses: *[Description]*
Project deliverables: *[Description]*
Project risks: *[Description]*
Project issues: *[Description]*
Project changes: *[Description]*

REVIEW DETAILS

Review category	Review question	Answer	Variance
Schedule	Was the phase completed to schedule?	Y/N	
Expenses	Was the phase completed within budgeted cost?	Y/N	
Deliverables: Deliverable # 1 Deliverable # 2 Deliverable # 3 Deliverable # 4 Deliverable # 5	*Deliverables:* Was Deliverable #1 completed and approved? Was Deliverable #2 completed and approved? Was Deliverable #3 completed and approved? Was Deliverable #4 completed and approved? Was Deliverable #5 completed and approved?	Y/N Y/N Y/N	
Risks	Are there any outstanding project risks?	Y/N	
Issues	Are there any outstanding project issues?	Y/N	
Changes	Are there any outstanding project changes?	Y/N	

APPROVAL DETAILS

Supporting documentation:
[Reference any supporting documentation used to substantiate the review details above.]

Project Sponsor Signature: _____ **Date:** __/__/__

THIS PROJECT HAS BEEN APPROVED TO PROCEED TO THE PROJECT CLOSURE PHASE

Figure 4.17 Phase review form for the execution phase

5

Project closure

5.1 INTRODUCTION

At the end of the execution phase, all required deliverables will have been constructed and accepted by the customer as complete. The project should have achieved the objectives and delivered the business benefits described in the business case. The project can be formally closed by undertaking the activities outlined in Figure 5.1.

It is no real surprise that most projects simply close their doors at this point. They release their resources and move on to other projects or business initiatives. In doing this, there is no formal review to determine whether the project actually achieved the objectives and business benefits stated in the business case. There is no clear indication of whether the project was a complete success or a marked failure.

In the author's experience, more than 90 per cent of projects undertaken fail to independently review the level of success after completion. The reason is simply that it takes time and additional budget to formally close the project and review its level of success. Also, many project managers are averse to having their project reviewed by an

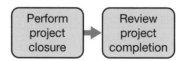

Figure 5.1   Project closure activities

external party to the project. This combined with the business expense incurred in seeking an independent review leads many businesses to overlook this phase and spend their budget on initiating other new project activities.

If you can find the time and budget to complete this phase in its entirety, you will not only ensure that your project is closed quickly and efficiently, but you will also gain the learning needed to ensure that your next project is even more successful than the last.

The following sections describe the activities required to perform project closure.

5.2 PERFORM PROJECT CLOSURE

To initiate the closure of the project, a project closure report should first be created. This report lists all of the closure activities and identifies the resource responsible for each activity listed. Following the approval of the report by the customer, the activities identified are actually undertaken to close the project.

Document a project closure report

A project closure report is a document which formalizes the closure of a project. It provides confirmation that the criteria for customer acceptance have been met and requests sign-off from the project sponsor to close the project. A project closure report includes:

- a detailed list of project completion criteria;
- confirmation that all completion criteria have been met;
- a list of outstanding business activities, risks and issues;
- a set of actions to hand over project deliverables and documentation, terminate supplier agreements, release resources to the business and inform stakeholders of the closure;
- A request for project closure approval.

A project closure report is prepared at the start of the project closure phase by the project manager and is submitted to the project sponsor for sign-off. Following sign-off, a suite of closure activities are undertaken to formally close out the project. The following sections describe how to create a project closure report, providing tables and real-life examples used for projects.

Validate the project completion

This section confirms that the criteria required to complete the project have been met and that any outstanding items have been identified.

Completion criteria

The first step towards initiating project closure is to confirm that the project completion criteria have been achieved. List the project completion criteria in Table 5.1 and for each criterion listed, confirm whether or not it has been approved by the customer.

Table 5.1 Completion criteria

Completion category	Completion criterion	Accepted by customer
Objectives	The project vision has been achieved as defined in the terms of reference All project objectives have been achieved as defined in the terms of reference	Y/N
Benefits	The full benefits have been realized, as defined in the business case	Y/N
Deliverables	All deliverables have been completed as defined in the terms of reference All deliverables have been accepted by the customer, as per the acceptance plan	Y/N
...	...	...

Outstanding items

Even though the project will have met the criteria for completion, there may be outstanding items which still need to be identified and undertaken. For each item, list the actions that should be taken and the owner responsible for each action, using Table 5.2.

Table 5.2 Completion actions

Item	Action	Owner
Activities	*List any outstanding activities or tasks*	*Name*
Risks	*List any business risks which have not yet been fully mitigated*	*Name*
Issues	*List any current issues which have not yet been resolved*	*Name*
...	...	...

Identify the closure activities

Next, identify the activities required to close the project. This includes the handover of deliverables and documentation to the customer, termination of supplier contracts, release of project resource back to the business or market place, and the communication of closure to all project stakeholders.

Deliverables

Create a plan for the release of all project deliverables to the customer, using Table 5.3.

Table 5.3   Deliverable release plan

Deliverable	Current		New		Hand-over plan		
Type	Owner	Location	Owner	Location	Activities	Date	Owner
Financial General Ledger, Accounts Payable and Accounts Receivable system modules	*Name*	*Address*	*Name*	*Address*	Hand over system maintenance activities. Hand over operational support activities. Hand over system documentation.	*Date*	*Name*
…	…	…	…	…	…	…	…

Documentation

Create a plan for the release of all project documentation to the customer, using Table 5.4.

Table 5.4 Documentation release plan

Documentation	Current		New		Hand-over plan		
Type	Owner	Location	Owner	Location	Activities	Date	Owner
Project initiation: Business case Feasibility study Terms of reference	*Name*	*Address*	*Name*	*Address*	*Activity*	*Date*	*Name*
Project planning: Project plan Resource plan Financial plan Quality plan Acceptance plan	*Name*	*Address*	*Name*	*Address*	*Activity*	*Date*	*Name*
Project execution: Change process Change form Change register Risk process Risk form Risk register	*Name*	*Address*	*Name*	*Address*	*Activity*	*Date*	*Name*
...	...	...	...	...	...	...	...

Suppliers

Create a plan for the termination of supplier contracts, using Table 5.5.

Table 5.5 Supplier termination

Supplier name	Contract reference	Termination activity	Release date	Activity owner
Supplier name	*Contract ref. no.*	Notify supplier of termination Return supplier assets Pay supplier invoices	*Date activity to be completed by*	Name of person responsible for activity
...	...	...	...	...

Resources

Create a plan for the release of all project resources, using Table 5.6.

Table 5.6 Resource release

Resource name	Current designation	Release activity	Release date	Activity owner
Staff name	*Project role*	Notify staff member of release. Release staff member. Return staff assets. Pay final staff salary.	*Date staff member released*	*Name of person responsible for activity*
Equipment name	*Equipment purpose*	Identify new owner. Sell/release equipment. Update General Ledger.	*Date equipment released*	*Name of person responsible for activity*
...	...	...	...	...

Communication

Identify a plan to communicate the project closure to all project stakeholders, using Table 5.7.

Table 5.7 Communications messages

Target audience	Intended message	Method used	Dispatch date	Dispatch owner
Recipient names or groups for receipt of messages	Project has been successfully completed and is now closed. All intended business benefits have been realized due to success of the project.	E-mail each project stakeholder. Final project board presentation.	*Date when communication should be released*	*Name of the person responsible for communication*
...	...	...	...	...

You are now ready to collate all of the materials listed in this section and create your project closure report. The next step in the project life cycle is to complete the project closure actions identified in the project closure report.

Complete project closure actions

Following approval, the activities stated in the project closure report are undertaken to close the project. These activities involve the hand-over of deliverables and documentation to the customer, the termination of supplier contracts, the release of project resource back to the business and the communication of project closure to all project stakeholders.

5.3 REVIEW PROJECT COMPLETION

The final step in the project life cycle is to review the project completion. A post-implementation review is undertaken to formally review the project and identify any lessons learnt.

Undertake a post-implementation review

A post-implementation review (PIR) is an assessment of the overall success of the project. The PIR is conducted by closely reviewing the project's performance against the original plans, and conformance against the project management processes defined for the project. The purpose of the PIR is not only to assess the project's level of success but also to identify lessons learnt and make recommendations for future projects to enhance their likelihood of success. The PIR results are recorded in a document which is retained by the business as the last record of the project.

The PIR document includes:

- an assessment of how the project performed against the objectives, scope, deliverables, schedule, expense and resource targets identified during the project initiation and project planning phases;
- a rating of the level of conformance against each of the project processes including time, cost, quality, change, risk, issue, procurement, communications and acceptance management;
- a list of the project achievements and failures;
- any lessons learnt and recommendations for future projects.

The PIR is undertaken at the end of the project closure phase, after the project closure report has been approved and all project closure activities completed. Some companies wait a number of weeks before undertaking the PIR, to enable the benefits provided by the project to be fully realized by the business. The PIR is typically completed by an independent person who offers an unbiased opinion of the project's level of success. The PIR is presented to the project sponsor/customer for approval and is retained on file for future projects.

Review project performance

To undertake a PIR, first identify how the project performed against each of the targets set during the initiation and planning phases of the project.

Benefits

Identify any deviations between the forecast business benefits specified in the business case and the actual benefits realized by the business, in Table 5.8.

Table 5.8   Benefit realization

Benefit category	Intended benefit	Forecast value	Actual value	Deviation
Financial	New revenue generated Reduction in costs Increased profit margin	x x x	x x x	x x x
Operational	Improved operational efficiency Reduction in produce time to market Enhanced quality of product/service	$x\%$ x hours $x\%$	$x\%$ x hours $x\%$	$x\%$ x hours $x\%$
Market	Increased market awareness Greater market share Additional competitive advantage	$x\%$ $x\%$ Describe	$x\%$ $x\%$ Describe	$x\%$ $x\%$ Describe
…	…	…	…	…

Objectives

Identify the extent to which the project achieved the objectives specified in the TOR, as well as any shortfall, in Table 5.9.

Table 5.9 Objectives achieved

Objective category	Original objective	Actual achievement	Shortfall
Business	• To deliver new accounts payable and receivable and payroll processes, thereby reducing financial processing timescales by at least 30%. • To build new work premises with 50% more space, 30 more car parks and 20% fewer operational costs than the existing premises. • To provide a new customer complaints service to enable customers to issue complaints online and receive a direct response from the company within 24 hours.	*Describe*	*Describe*
Technology	• To install a new accounts payable, receivable and payroll system, resulting in a 20% improvement in accounting efficiencies. • To relocate existing technology infrastructure at the new building premises within a 2-month timeframe with no impact on customer service delivery. • To build a new website allowing customers to track customer complaints.	*Describe*	*Describe*
...	...	...	...

Scope

Identify whether at any stage, the project deviated from the original scope defined in the terms of reference, in Table 5.10.

Table 5.10 Scope conformance

Scope category	Original scope	Actual scope	Deviation
Processes	*Describe*	*Describe*	*Describe*
Organizational areas			
Locations			
Data			
Applications			
Technologies			
...	...	...	...

Deliverables

List the original deliverables, quality criteria and standards outlined in the quality plan and rate the overall level of achievement for each, using Table 5.11.

Table 5.11 Resultant deliverables

Deliverable	Quality criteria	Quality standards	% achieved
Oracle Financials General Ledger (GL), Accounts Payable (AP) and Accounts Receivable (AR) system modules	*System functionality:* • GL tested and installed. • AP tested and installed. • AR tested and installed. *System performance:* • System up-time • System response time. • Data migrated.	*System functionality:* • GL operational (no errors). • AP operational (no errors). • AR operational (no errors). *System performance:* • < 5 second response times. • 100% data accuracy.	*0–100%*
...	...	...	...

Schedule

Compare the actual delivery schedule with the planned delivery schedule as documented in the project plan, in Figure 5.2.

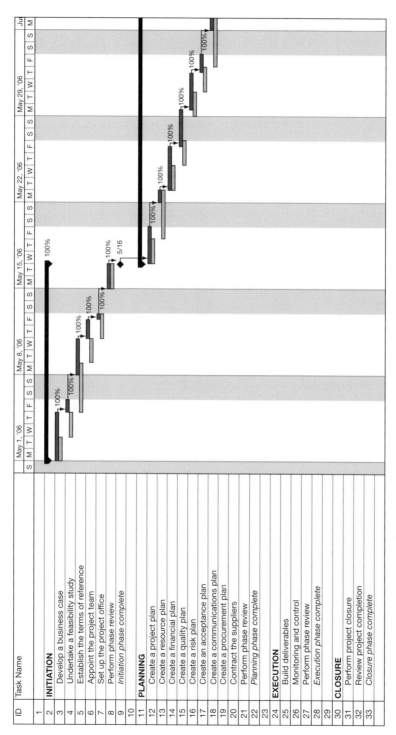

ID	Task Name
1	
2	**INITIATION**
3	Develop a business case
4	Undertake a feasibility study
5	Establish the terms of reference
6	Appoint the project team
7	Set up the project office
8	Perform phase review
9	*Initiation phase complete*
10	
11	**PLANNING**
12	Create a project plan
13	Create a resource plan
14	Create a financial plan
15	Create a quality plan
16	Create a risk plan
17	Create an acceptance plan
18	Create a communications plan
19	Create a procurement plan
20	Contract the suppliers
21	Perform phase review
22	*Planning phase complete*
23	
24	**EXECUTION**
25	Build deliverables
26	Monitoring and control
27	Perform phase review
28	*Execution phase complete*
29	
30	**CLOSURE**
31	Perform project closure
32	Review project completion
33	*Closure phase complete*

Figure 5.2 Actual delivery schedule

Expenses

Identify any deviations between the forecast project expenditure and the actual project expenditure, as documented in the financial plan.

Table 5.12   Final expenditure

Expense type	Forecast expenditure	Actual expenditure	Deviation
Labour: Project manager *Labour type*	*$/£/other currency*	*$/£/other currency*	*$/£/other currency*
Equipment: Computers *Equipment type*			
Materials: Stationery *Material type*			
Other:			
Grand total			

Resources

Compare the quantity of resource forecast with the quantity of resource actually utilized (from the resource plan), using Table 5.13.

Table 5.13   Final resource utilization

Resource type	Forecast resource level	Actual resource level	Deviation
Labour: Project manager *Labour type*	*$/£/other currency*	*$/£/other currency*	*$/£/other currency*
Equipment: Computer *Equipment type*			
Materials: Printer cartridges *Materials type*			
Other:			
Grand total			

Review project conformance

Next, identify whether or not the project conformed to the processes outlined during the initiation and planning phases. A number of checklists have been provided to help you determine the actual level of conformance.

Time management process

Use Table 5.14.

Table 5.14   Time management conformance

Checklist	Y/N
Was a clear schedule outlined in the project plan?	Y/N
Did the schedule include all activities, tasks and dependencies?	
Were clear resource estimates outlined in the project plan?	
Did all staff regularly record time using a timesheet?	
Was the project manager required to approve all timesheets?	
Were any timesheet issues raised by the project manager?	
Was timesheet information recorded in the project plan?	
Was additional time required for any activity over that planned?	
Were there any activities recorded with no time against them?	

Cost management process

Use Table 5.15.

Table 5.15   Cost management conformance

Checklist	Y/N
Were all expense types identified in the financial plan?	*Y/N*
Were all expenses adequately quantified in the financial plan?	
Did the project actually incur all expenses planned?	
Were expense forms completed for all project expenses?	
Were invoices and receipts kept for expenses incurred?	
Was the project manager required to approve all project expenses?	
Were the approval procedures diligently followed?	
Were all expenses recorded in an expense register?	
Was the expense register monitored to assess total expenditure?	
Did the project spend more than the original budget?	
Was the project board required to allocate additional funding?	
Was the customer satisfied with the overall level of expenditure?	

Quality management process
Use Table 5.16.

Table 5.16   Quality management conformance

Checklist	Y/N
Were all project deliverables identified in the quality plan?	*Y/N*
Were clear quality targets identified?	
Were quality criteria and standards specified?	
Were clear quality assurance techniques identified?	
Did regular quality assurance reviews take place?	
Were clear quality control techniques identified?	
Did regular quality control take place?	
Were quality management roles formally defined?	
Did staff operate according to their defined quality role?	
Were all deliverables recorded in a quality register?	
Were quality review forms completed for all quality reviews?	
Were quality deviations formally tracked?	
Were quality improvements actions actually undertaken?	

Change management process

Use Table 5.17.

Table 5.17 Change management conformance

Checklist	Y/N
Were all changes managed through the formal change process?	Y/N
Were change request forms completed for all changes?	
Were change request forms reviewed by the change manager?	
Were feasibility studies undertaken for any appropriate changes?	
Did anyone other than the approval group approve any changes?	
Were all approved changes implemented as required?	
Were change management roles formally defined?	
Did staff operate according to their defined change role?	
Were all changes recorded within a change register?	
Did any change impact on the business in an unexpected manner?	
Did any change result in a new risk or issue?	
Did any changes result in a new business benefit or cost?	
Were all changes applied prior to project closure?	

Risk management process

Use Table 5.18.

Table 5.18 Risk management conformance

Checklist	Y/N
Were all important project risks identified early in the project?	*Y/N*
Were all risks managed through a formal risk process?	
Were risk forms completed for all important risks identified?	
Were all risk forms reviewed by the project manager?	
Were the risk likelihood and impact ratings assigned appropriately?	
Was a clear mitigation plan outlined for each risk identified?	
Were risk mitigating actions assigned appropriately for action?	
Were risk mitigating actions completed accordingly?	
Were risk management roles formally defined?	
Did staff operate according to their defined risk role?	
Were all risks recorded in a risk register?	
Did any risk result in a change request?	
Did any risk actually eventuate and impact on the project?	

Issue management process
Use Table 5.19.

Table 5.19   Issue management conformance

Checklist	Y/N
Were all project issues identified during the project?	*Y/N*
Were all issues managed through a formal issue process?	
Were issue forms completed for all issues identified?	
Did issue forms describe the impact of the issue on the project?	
Were all issue forms reviewed by the project manager?	
Were clear recommended actions identified to resolve the issue?	
Did the project review group review all issue forms?	
Were all recommended actions undertaken accordingly?	
Were issue management roles formally defined?	
Did staff operate according to their assigned issue role?	
Were all issues recorded in an issue register?	
Did any issue remain unresolved throughout the project?	
Did any issue result in the identification of a new project risk?	
Did any issue result in a lower quality deliverable being produced?	

Procurement management process
Use Table 5.20.

Table 5.20 Procurement management conformance

Checklist	Y/N
Was a formal process undertaken to select preferred suppliers?	*Y/N*
Was the supplier evaluation process undertaken in a fair manner?	
Were detailed contracts signed with all suppliers?	
Were all suppliers provided with a statement of work (SOW)?	
Were formal supplier performance reviews regularly undertaken?	
Were all supplier issues raised with the project manager?	
Were all supplier issues resolved appropriately?	
Were all supplier issues recorded in an issue register?	
Did any supplier issues remain unresolved throughout the project?	
Did any supplier issues result in a new project risk?	
Did any supplier issues lower the quality of deliverables?	
Were clear payment milestones identified for each supplier?	
Were any supplier contracts terminated before the planned end date?	
Did any legal issues result from the supplier performance, payment milestones or contract termination?	

Communications management process

Use Table 5.21.

Table 5.21 Communications management conformance

Checklist	Y/N
Did the communications plan clearly identify the intended target audience, message and methods to be used?	*Y/N*
Were regular reports distributed to key project stakeholders?	
Did the status reports clearly identify progress, risks and issues?	
Were the project board kept regularly informed of progress?	
Were the project team kept regularly informed of progress?	
Was the customer kept regularly informed of progress?	
Was there a clear escalation path for urgent project matters?	
Were all project decisions clearly documented and communicated?	
Was the project closure clearly communicated to all stakeholders?	
Were any communication issues identified?	
Did any communication issues result in new project risks?	
Did any communication issues affect the ability of the project to meet its stated objectives?	
Were the project board and customer expectations well managed?	
Was the project perceived to be a success?	

Acceptance management process

Use Table 5.22.

Table 5.22 Acceptance management conformance

Checklist	Y/N
Were clear acceptance criteria outlined in the acceptance plan?	*Y/N*
Was customer acceptance requested for all completed deliverables?	
Was an acceptance form completed for each deliverable?	
Were acceptance reviews undertaken for each deliverable?	
Was the customer involved in all acceptance reviews?	
Were the acceptance reviews adequate?	
Were the review results formally recorded in an acceptance register?	
Has the customer formally accepted all deliverables?	
Were acceptance management roles formally defined?	
Did staff operate according to their defined acceptance role?	

Identify project achievements

List the major achievements for this project and describe the positive effect that each achievement has had on the customer's business, using Table 5.23.

Table 5.23 Project achievements

Achievement	Effect on business
Description of the achievement	*Description of the positive effect that the achievement has had on the business*
…	…

List project failures

List any project failures and describe the effect that they have had on the customer's business, using Table 5.24.

Table 5.24 Project failures

Failure	Effect on business
Description of the failure	*Description of the effect that the failure has had on the business*
...	...

Document project lessons learnt

Describe the lessons learnt from undertaking this project and list any recommendations for similar projects in the future, using Table 5.25.

Table 5.25 Lessons learnt

Learning	Recommendation
Description of the lesson learnt	*Recommendations for similar future projects*
...	...

You are now ready to collate all of the materials listed in this section and create your post-implementation review for approval. This is the final step in the project closure phase and completes our detailed walk-though of the project management life cycle.

6

Epilogue

And there you have it, the project management life cycle in a nutshell. I hope by now that you have gained a detailed understanding of the Method123® Project Management Methodology (MPMM) by learning the phases, activities and tasks required to undertake a project. Here are some final tips for success.

PROJECT INITIATION

- Always create a business case. You will not only create a sound basis for the initiation of the project, but you will also set expectations for delivery. If you deliver the project to meet these expectations, then you have achieved success.
- Gain confidence that your project will deliver a feasible solution by undertaking a feasibility study early in the project life cycle.
- Avoid 'scope creep' by properly documenting the terms of reference.
- Take the time to find suitably skilled staff with the correct level of experience. Remember that 'Great projects are delivered by great people'.
- Make sure that your project team have the tools, equipment and facilities needed to complete the project by establishing a professional project office environment.

PROJECT PLANNING

- Create a project plan listing every activity and task required to deliver the project.
- Make sure you have right resource at the right time, by documenting a resource plan.
- Manage expenses wisely, using a comprehensive financial plan.
- Identify quality targets, quality reviews and quality control methods using a quality plan.
- Mitigate project risks from the outset by creating a detailed risk plan.
- Define the customer acceptance criteria early in an acceptance plan.
- Create a communications plan to identify communications events and processes.
- Use a procurement plan to identify products to be sourced from outside the project.
- Contract preferred suppliers by undertaking a formal tender management process.

PROJECT EXECUTION

- Build your project deliverables in accordance with the project plan at all times.
- Use the following project management processes to monitor and control the creation of deliverables within the project:
    - time management;
    - cost management;
    - quality management;
    - change management;
    - risk management;
    - issue management;
    - procurement management;
    - acceptance management;
    - communications management.

PROJECT CLOSURE

- Close the project formally by documenting and executing a project closure report.
- Allow an independent resource to review the level of project success and identify any lessons learnt for future projects.

To gain the maximum benefit from using MPMM, consider customizing it to suit your project environment by selecting the activities in the life cycle that you feel are most relevant. The methodology is fully scalable, meaning that you can pick and choose the activities that best suit your needs and still have a robust framework from which to deliver projects. By selecting the activities which are most relevant to your particular project environment you can use this methodology to undertake any size of project, in any industry.

It's comforting to know that more than 45,000 managers, consultants, trainers, lecturers and students in 50 different countries use MPMM to undertake their projects. If you would like to know more about MPMM, please visit www.method123.com where you will find a complete suite of project management tools to complement all of the activities described in this book. By using these tools, you will save time and money by not having to start projects from scratch.

By adopting MPMM as your project management methodology, you will dramatically increase your chances of project success.

I wish you all the very best.

Kind regards,

Jason Westland
CEO, Method123® Ltd

Appendix

ACTIVITY MODEL

Figure A.1 lists all the activities in the project management life cycle.

DOCUMENTS

Table A.1 lists the documents created by project managers during the project management life cycle.

See www.method123.com for a complete set of project management templates, to help you create all of the documents outlined in this book.

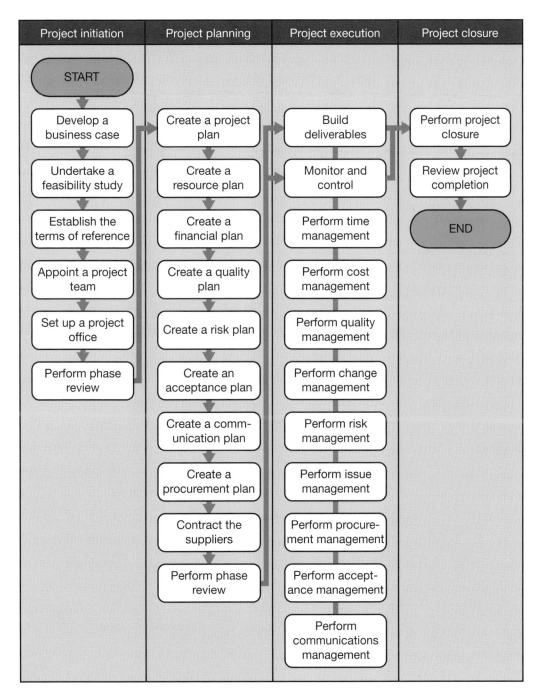

Figure A.1 Project life cycle activity model

Table A.1 Project documents

Phase	Activity	Document
Initiation	Develop a business case	Business case
	Undertake a feasibility study	Feasibility study
	Establish the terms of reference	Terms of reference
	Appoint the project team	Job description
	Set up the project office	Project office checklist
	Perform a phase review	Phase review form
Planning	Create a project plan	Project plan
	Create a resource plan	Resource plan
	Create a financial plan	Financial plan
	Create a quality plan	Quality plan
	Create a risk plan	Risk plan
	Create an acceptance plan	Acceptance plan
	Create a communications plan	Communications plan
	Create a procurement plan	Procurement plan
	Contract the suppliers	Tender management process Statement of work (SOW) Request for information (RFI) Request for proposal (RFP) Supplier contract Tender register
	Perform a phase review	Phase review form

Table A.1 *continued*

Phase	Activity	Document
Execution	Build deliverables	n/a
	Monitor and control	
	Perform time management	Time management process Timesheet form Timesheet register
	Perform cost management	Cost management process Expense form Expense register
	Perform quality management	Quality management process Quality review form Quality register
	Perform change management	Change management process Change form Change register
	Perform risk management	Risk management process Risk form Risk register
	Perform issue management	Issue management process Issue form Issue register
	Perform procurement management	Procurement management process Purchase order form Procurement register
	Perform acceptance management	Acceptance management process Acceptance form Acceptance register
	Perform communications management	Communications management process Project status report Communications register
	Perform a phase review	Phase review form
Closure	Perform a project closure	Project closure report
	Review project completion	Post-implementation review

Glossary

ABBREVIATIONS

The following acronyms have been used in this book:

CAPEX	capital expenditure
CRF	change request form
OPEX	operational expenditure
PIR	post-implementation review
QA	quality assurance
QC	quality control
RFI	Request for information
RFP	request for proposal
SOW	statement of work
TOR	terms of reference

DEFINITIONS

The following definitions apply to terminology used in this book:

acceptance management   The process by which deliverables produced by the project are reviewed and accepted by the customer.

acceptance planning   The process of identifying the milestones, criteria and standards for the acceptance of deliverables by the customer.

business case   A document outlining the justification for initiation of a project. It includes a description of the business problem or opportunity, a list of the available solution options, their associated costs and benefits and a preferred solution for approval.

change management   The process by which changes to the project scope, deliverables, timescales or resources are defined, evaluated and approved prior to implementation.
communications management   The process by which communications messages are identified, created, reviewed and dispatched within a project.
communications planning   The process of identifying the type and regularity of information to be dispatched to project stakeholders, to keep them informed of the progress of a project.
cost management   The process by which costs/expenses incurred on a project are formally identified, approved and paid.

deliverable   A quantifiable outcome of a project which results in the partial or full achievement of the project objectives.
dependency   A logical relationship between two or more project activities. The four types of dependencies are: start-to-finish, start-to-start, finish-to-start, finish-to-finish.

feasibility study   A document that identifies each of the solution options to a particular business problem or opportunity and assesses the likelihood of each option achieving the desired outcome of a project.
financial planning   The process of identifying, describing and quantifying the financial resources required to undertake a project.

issue   Events that are currently affecting the ability of a project to produce the required deliverables.
issue management   The process by which issues are formally identified, communicated, monitored and resolved.

job description   A document which describes a particular role and set of responsibilities in a project.

milestone   The recognition of an important event within a project, usually the achievement of a key project deliverable.

phase review   A checkpoint at the end of each project phase to ensure that a project has achieved its stated objectives and deliverables as planned.

procurement management The process by which products are sourced from preferred suppliers. This also includes the process of managing each preferred supplier relationship on an ongoing basis.

procurement planning The process of identifying, describing and quantifying the products to be sourced externally to a project.

product A good or service that is acquired from an external supplier to assist with the production of a project deliverable.

project A unique endeavour to produce a set of deliverables within clearly specified time, cost and quality constraints.

project activity A set of tasks which usually result in the partial or full completion of a project deliverable.

project life cycle A series of phases which are undertaken to deliver a required project outcome.

project management The skills, tools and management processes required to successfully undertake a project.

project office The physical premises within which a project team reside.

project phase A set of project activities and tasks which usually result in the completion of a project deliverable.

project plan A document that lists the phases, activities, tasks, timeframes and resources required to complete a project.

project schedule A series of planned dates within which activities and tasks must be completed to achieve project milestones.

project task A specific work item to be undertaken which usually results in the partial completion of a project deliverable.

project team A group of people who report to a project manager for the purpose of delivering a project.

quality The extent to which the final deliverable conforms to the customer requirements.

quality assurance The preventative steps taken to eliminate any variances in the quality of deliverables produced from the quality targets set.

quality control The curative steps taken to eliminate any variances in the quality of deliverables produced from the quality targets set.

quality management The process by which the quality of the deliverables and management processes is assured and controlled for a project, using quality assurance and quality control techniques.

quality planning The process of identifying the approach to be taken to ensure and control the quality of the deliverables and management processes within a project.

request for information A document that is issued to potential suppliers to enable them to provide summarized information describing how they will meet the procurement requirements of a project.

request for proposal A document that is issued to a short-listed group of suppliers to enable them to submit a detailed proposal defining how they will meet the procurement requirements of a project.

resource The labour, equipment and materials used to undertake a project.

resource planning The process of identifying, describing and quantifying the resources required to complete a project.

risk Any event which is likely to adversely affect the ability of the project to achieve the defined objectives.

risk management The process within which risks are formally identified, quantified and managed during a project.

risk mitigation A set of actions to be taken to avoid, transfer or mitigate risks, based on their priority. This includes the preventive actions to be taken during the project to reduce the likelihood of the risk occurring as well as the contingent actions to be taken to reduce the impact on the project should the risk occur.

risk planning The process of identifying the approach to be taken to mitigate risks within a project.

scope The total aggregation of deliverables produced by a project.

solution A set of deliverables which once combined, solve a particular business problem or realize a particular business opportunity.

statement of work A document that defines the procurement requirements of the project in sufficient enough detail to enable potential suppliers to determine if they are able to meet those requirements.

supplier contract An agreement between a project team and an external supplier for the acquisition of a defined set of products to meet the procurement requirements of the project.

tender document A formal document issued to suppliers during the tender process to enable them to provide the project team with the confidence that they can meet the procurement needs of the project. The request for information and request for proposal are both examples of tender documents.

tender management The process by which interested suppliers are identified, evaluated and selected for the supply of products (goods or services) to a project.

terms of reference A document that outlines the purpose of the project, the manner in which the project will be structured and how it will be implemented.

time management The process of recording and quantifying time spent completing tasks on a project.

Index

NB: page numbers in *italic* indicate figures or tables